Thank you and goodnight! Sir Alex Ferguson picks up the 2012-13 Premier League trophy after announcing his retirement from Manchester United

CONTENTS

Your guide to the best players, biggest legends, top competitions and the winners of all the major football events on the planet. Statistics are correct until the end of season 2012-13, except where indicated. Where figures are disputed we have relied on clubs and historians for

Pedigree

Published 2013. Pedigree Books Limited, Beech Hill House, Walnut Gardens, Exeter, Devon EX4 4DH. The Pedigree trademark, email and website addresses, are the sole and exclusive properties of Pedigree Group Limited, used under licence in this publication. © 2013 Pedigree Group Limited www.pedigreebooks.com *Shoot* ® is a registered trademark of Pedigree Group Limited shoot@pedigreegroup.co.uk

Records are there to be broken – the problem is that most of football's high spots are currently occupied by Lionel Messi!

The Barcelona and Argentina forward currently collects more silverware than any other player on the planet… and shows no signs of easing up on his amazing journey through the game.

There's no doubt he's won a few more titles and accolades before you even reach the end of this book, but here are just some of the awards that have probably meant he's had to build an extension to his home in which to store the honours!

MESSI THE

Lionel Messi holds up the Ballon d'Or following his fourth victory in a row

1 World Player of the Year (2009)

4 Ballon d'Or as the world's best footballer (2009, 2010, 2011,

6 La Liga titles (2005, 2006, 2009, 2010, 2011, 2013)

2 Copa del Rey (2009, 2012)

5 Supercopa de Espana (2005, 2006, 2009, 2010, 2011)

3 Champions Leagues (2006, 2009, 2011)

2 UEFA Super Cups (2009, 2011)

2 FIFA Club World Cup (2009, 2011)

MAGICIAN!

3 European Golden Shoe (2010, 2012, 2013)

7 Argentina Footballer of the Year (2005, 2007, 2008, 2009, 2010, 2011, 2012)

1 Olympic Gold (2008)

1 FIFA Under-20 World Cup (2005)

4 Champions League top scorer (2009, 2010, 2011, 2012)

1 Copa del Rey top scorer (2011)

3 La Liga Player of the Year (2009, 2010, 2011)

91 Most goals scored in one calendar year

79 Most club goals in one year

73 Most club goals in one season

50 Most La Liga goals in a season

25 Most international goals in one year (club and country)

12 Most international goals in one year (country)

19 Consecutive games scored in (30 goals)

8 Most La Liga hat-tricks in a season

Extra-Time

Messi is also Barcelona's record scorer – with a host of other scoring records to his name. We won't list them all as he's probably broken them or on his way to breaking them already!

TOP GROUNDS

More than 250 football grounds around the world have the capacity to cater for over 40,000 fans.

It's no surprise that some of the biggest stadiums are for countries' national sides but there are many club grounds in Europe that can hold big crowds.

Total capacities are constantly changing due to ground developments and health and safety rules.

10 BIGGEST NATIONAL STADIA

1. **INDIA,** Salt Lake, 120,000
2. **IRAN,** Azadi, 100,000
3. **MEXICO,** Estadio Azteca, 105,000
4. **SOUTH AFRICA,** FNB, 94,700
5. **ENGLAND,** Wembley, 90,000
6. **INDONESIA,** Gelora Bung Karno, 88,300
7. **MALAYSIA,** Bukit Jalil, 87,400
8. **EGYPT,** Borg El Arab, 86,000
9. **AUSTRALIA,** ANZ, 83,500
10. **BRAZIL,** Maracana, 82,200

But we've listed some of the best and most famous grounds in Europe where top teams play – and which are dream destinations for many professional players.

Allianz Arena

WHERE Munich
TEAMS Bayern Munich, TSV 1860
CAPACITY 71,100
OPENED 2005

The Alliance Arena was used for the 2006 World Cup and also hosted the Champions League Final in 2012.

Amsterdam Arena

WHERE Amsterdam
TEAM Ajax
CAPACITY 53,000
OPENED 1996

Venue for the 2013 Europa League Final, the Arena also hosted games in the European Championships of 2000.

Bernabeu

WHERE Madrid

TEAM Real Madrid

CAPACITY 85,400

OPENED 1947

The Santiago Bernabeu has expanded its capacity over the years and has hosted European Cup Finals and games in the 1982 World Cup.

Borussia-
Park

WHERE Monchengladbach

TEAM Borussia Monchengladbach

CAPACITY 54,000

OPENED 2004

Although it missed out on being used for the 2006 World Cup, the stadium was a venue for the 2011 Women's World Cup and hosted a semi-final.

Camp Nou

WHERE Barcelona
TEAM Barcelona
CAPACITY 99,700
OPENED 1957

Used for the 1992 Olympics and Champions League Finals, the Camp Nou has also hosted international games.

Celtic Park

WHERE Glasgow
TEAM Celtic
CAPACITY 60,300
OPENED 1892

The stadium, also known as Parkhead, has been vastly renovated and been used for numerous major finals and even Scotland internationals when the country's Hampden Park has not been available.

Emirates Stadium

WHERE London
TEAM Arsenal
CAPACITY 60,200
OPENED 2006

Just a short walk from the Gunners' former home at Highbury, the Ashburton Grove ground is the second-biggest club football stadium in England.

Estadio da Luz

WHERE Lisbon
TEAM Benfica
CAPACITY 65,600
OPENED 2003

Better known as the Stadium of Light, played host to games in Euro 2004 and has been chosen as the venue for the 2014 Champions League Final.

Estadio Jose Alvalade

WHERE Lisbon
TEAM Sporting Portugal
CAPACITY 50,000
OPENED 2003

Venue for Euro 2004 games and the 2005 UEFA Cup Final, this is the second stadium of the same name. The original one was built in 1956.

Ibrox

WHERE Glasgow
TEAM Rangers
CAPACITY 51,000
OPENED 1899

Rebuilt a number of times, Ibrox holds the record for the biggest crowd at a British football game, a staggering 118,567 for a league clash with Celtic in 1939.

Luzhniki Stadium

WHERE Moscow

TEAM Spartak and CSKA Moscow

CAPACITY 89,300

OPENED 1956

A venue for the 2018 World Cup, the Luzhniki has a FIFA-approved artificial pitch. The venue hosted the 2008 Champions League Final.

Old Trafford

WHERE Manchester

TEAM Manchester United

CAPACITY 75,700

OPENED 1910

Much developed since it first opened, Old Trafford is the biggest club football ground in the UK and is nicknamed the Theatre of Dreams. It has staged internationals and the 2003 Champions League Final.

St. James' Park

WHERE Newcastle
TEAM Newcastle United
CAPACITY 52,300
OPENED 1892

Now unrecognisable from its original state due to redevelopment that began in 1998, St. James' is the third-largest club ground in England. It played host to Olympic football in 2012 and has staged internationals.

San Siro

WHERE Milan
TEAMS AC and Inter Milan
CAPACITY 80,000
OPENED 1926

The Stadio Giuseppe Meazza, named after a double World Cup-winner, hosts Milan's rival clubs and has been the venue for Italy international games in both football and rugby.

Westfalenstadion

WHERE Dortmund
TEAM Borussia Dortmund
CAPACITY 80,700
OPENED 1974

The biggest ground in Germany opened in time to stage 1974 World Cup games. It also hosted the finals of 2006.

Stade Velodrome

WHERE Marseille
TEAM Olympique Marseille
CAPACITY 42,000
OPENED 1937

Last renovated in 1998, the Velodrome is expected to increase its capacity to 67,000 in time for Euro 2016. It was used in the 1938 World Cup Finals.

Stadio Olimpico

WHERE Rome
TEAMS Roma, Lazio
CAPACITY 82,300
OPENED 1936

The venue for the final of Coppa Italia, rugby and Italy's national athletics stadium, the Olimpico has hosted European Championship games and European Cup Finals.

Sukru Saracoglu

WHERE Istanbul
TEAM Fenerbache
CAPACITY 50,500
OPENED 1908

Renovated in 1999 and 2006, the ground hosted the UEFA Cup Final of 2009 and is on the site of the first-ever football game to be played in Turkey.

Veltins- Arena

WHERE Gelsenkirchen
TEAM Schalke 04
CAPACITY 78,900
OPENED 2001

Venue of the 2004 Champions League Final and for games in World Cup 2006, the Veltins has a roof that closes and a pitch that can be moved outside to allow the grass to grow.

Vicente Calderon Stadium

WHERE Madrid
TEAM Atletico Madrid
CAPACITY 54,900
OPENED 1966

Named after a former club president, the Calderon was used for games in the 1982 World Cup and has been a venue for the Spanish national side.

The World's Biggest-Earning Football Teams

A number of football clubs may be facing financial meltdown but the big boys keep on getting bigger! Whilst some sides struggle to even make ends meet, financial experts reckon Manchester United are the most valuable side in the world, worth an estimated £1.9 BILLION!

That puts the 13 times English Premier League champions ahead of the likes of Real Madrid and Barcelona.

But when it comes to the latest figures for how much income clubs have pulled in, the Spanish giants move ahead of the Red Devils.

Top 20 Earners

1 Real Madrid
£414.7m

2 Barcelona
£390.8m

3 Manchester United
£320.3m

4 Bayern Munich
£298.1m

5 Chelsea
£261m

6 Arsenal
£234.9m

7 Manchester City
£231.1m

8 AC Milan
£207.9m

9 Liverpool
£188.7m

10 Juventus
£158.1m

11 Borussia Dortmund
£153m

12 Inter
£150.4m

13 Tottenham
£144.2m

14 Schalke
£141.2m

15 Napoli
£120.1m

16 Marseille
£109.8m

17 Lyon
£106.7m

18 Hamburg
£98m

19 Roma
£93.8m

20 Newcastle
£93.3m

Deloitte's Football Money League

PREMIER LEAGUE

English football's top tier was known as Division One from 1892, having previously been just one division.

From 1992-93 it became known as the Premiership, the forerunner to what we now call the Barclays Premier League.

The Premiership had 22 founding members. These included Ipswich Town and Middlesbrough, who had been promoted from the old Second Division, along with Blackburn Rovers who won that division's play-off final.

The other founders were the rest of the teams from Division One, who had broken away from the Football League.

Luton Town, Notts County and West Ham missed out on the chance of taking part in the Premiership as they had been relegated from the old Division One.

2009-10

ALL THE WINNERS...

1992-93	Manchester United
1993-94	Manchester United
1994-95	Blackburn Rovers
1995-96	Manchester United
1996-97	Manchester United
1997-98	Arsenal
1998-99	Manchester United
1999-00	Manchester United
2000-01	Manchester United
2001-02	Arsenal
2002-03	Manchester United
2003-04	Arsenal
2004-05	Chelsea
2005-06	Chelsea
2006-07	Manchester United
2007-08	Manchester United
2008-09	Manchester United
2009-10	Chelsea
2010-11	Manchester United
2011-12	Manchester City
2012-13	Manchester United

FOOTBALL LEAGUE 1888-1892

1889	Preston North End
1890	Preston North End
1891	Everton
1892	Sunderland

DIVISION ONE 1893-1992

1893	Sunderland
1894	Aston Villa
1895	Sunderland
1896	Aston Villa
1897	Aston Villa
1898	Sheffield United
1899	Aston Villa
1900	Aston Villa
1901	Liverpool
1902	Sunderland
1903	The Wednesday

Year	Champion	Year	Champion
1904	The Wednesday	1953	Arsenal
1905	Newcastle United	1954	Wolverhampton Wanderers
1906	Liverpool	1955	Chelsea
1907	Newcastle United	1956	Manchester United
1908	Manchester United	1957	Manchester United
1909	Newcastle United	1958	Wolverhampton Wanderers
1910	Aston Villa	1959	Wolverhampton Wanderers
1911	Manchester United	1960	Burnley
1912	Blackburn Rovers	1961	Tottenham
1913	Sunderland	1962	Ipswich Town
1914	Blackburn Rovers	1963	Everton
1915	Everton	1964	Liverpool
1916-1919	World War I	1965	Manchester United
1920	West Bromwich Albion	1966	Liverpool
1921	Burnley	1967	Manchester United
1922	Liverpool	1968	Manchester City
1923	Liverpool	1969	Leeds United
1924	Huddersfield Town	1970	Everton
1925	Huddersfield Town	1971	Arsenal
1926	Huddersfield Town	1972	Derby County
1927	Newcastle United	1973	Liverpool
1928	Everton	1974	Leeds United
1929	Sheffield Wednesday	1975	Derby County
1930	Sheffield Wednesday	1976	Liverpool
1931	Arsenal	1977	Liverpool
1932	Everton	1978	Nottingham Forest
1933	Arsenal	1979	Liverpool
1934	Arsenal	1980	Liverpool
1935	Arsenal	1981	Aston Villa
1936	Sunderland	1982	Liverpool
1937	Manchester City	1983	Liverpool
1938	Arsenal	1984	Liverpool
1939	Everton	1985	Everton
1940-46	World War II	1986	Liverpool
1947	Liverpool	1987	Everton
1948	Arsenal	1988	Liverpool
1949	Portsmouth	1989	Arsenal
1950	Portsmouth	1990	Liverpool
1951	Tottenham	1991	Arsenal
1952	Manchester United	1992	Leeds United

CHAMPIONSHIP

The Championship, English football's second tier, has also been called Division Two and Division One. From 1892 until the birth of the Premier League in 1992-93 it was Division Two, then it became Division One. The division changed its name to The Championship in 2004.

ALL THE WINNERS...

DIVISION TWO WINNERS (1893-1992)

1893	Small Heath
1894	Liverpool
1895	Bury
1896	Liverpool
1897	Notts County
1898	Burnley
1899	Manchester City
1900	The Wednesday
1901	Grimsby Town
1902	West Bromwich Albion
1903	Manchester City
1904	Preston North End
1905	Liverpool
1906	Bristol City
1907	Nottingham Forest
1908	Bradford City
1909	Bolton Wanderers
1910	Manchester City
1911	West Bromwich Albion
1912	Derby County
1913	Preston North End
1914	Notts County
1915	Derby County
1915-19	World War I
1920	Tottenham
1921	Birmingham City
1922	Nottingham Forest
1923	Notts County
1924	Leeds United
1925	Leicester City
1926	Sheffield Wednesday
1927	Middlesbrough
1928	Manchester City
1929	Middlesbrough
1930	Blackpool
1931	Everton
1932	Wolverhampton Wanderers
1933	Stoke City
1934	Grimsby Town
1935	Brentford
1936	Manchester United
1937	Leicester City
1938	Aston Villa
1939	Blackburn Rovers
1939-46	World War II
1947	Manchester City
1948	Birmingham City
1949	Fulham
1950	Tottenham
1951	Preston North End
1952	Sheffield Wednesday
1953	Sheffield United
1954	Leicester City
1955	Birmingham City
1956	Sheffield Wednesday
1957	Leicester City
1958	West Ham
1959	Sheffield Wednesday

1960	Aston Villa		**1990**	Leeds United
1961	Ipswich Town		**1991**	Oldham Athletic
1962	Liverpool		**1992**	Ipswich Town
1963	Stoke City			
1964	Leeds United			

DIVISION ONE WINNERS (1993-2004)

1965	Newcastle United			
1966	Manchester City		**1993**	Newcastle United
1967	Coventry City		**1994**	Crystal Palace
1968	Ipswich Town		**1995**	Middlesbrough
1969	Derby County		**1996**	Sunderland
1970	Huddersfield Town		**1997**	Bolton Wanderers
1971	Leicester City		**1998**	Nottingham Forest
1972	Norwich City		**1999**	Sunderland
1973	Burnley		**2000**	Charlton Athletic
1974	Middlesbrough		**2001**	Fulham
1975	Manchester United		**2002**	Manchester City
1976	Sunderland		**2003**	Portsmouth
1977	Wolverhampton Wanderers		**2004**	Norwich City
1978	Bolton Wanderers			

CHAMPIONSHIP WINNERS (2005-12)

1979	Crystal Palace			
1980	Leicester City		**2005**	Sunderland
1981	West Ham		**2006**	Reading
1982	Luton Town		**2007**	Sunderland
1983	Queens Park Rangers		**2008**	West Bromwich Albion
1984	Chelsea		**2009**	Wolverhampton Wanderers
1985	Oxford United		**2010**	Newcastle United
1986	Norwich City		**2011**	Queens Park Rangers
1987	Derby County		**2012**	Reading
1988	Millwall		**2013**	Cardiff City
1989	Chelsea			

LEAGUE ONE

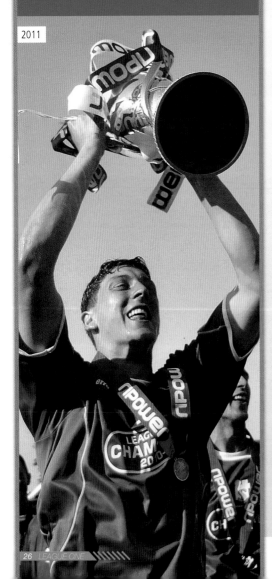

2011

T he third level of English league football has also been known as **Division Two and Division Three.**
This level began life as Division Three in 1920 for just one season. It then split into regional leagues, Division Three North and South until 1958.

It reverted back to one national Division Three until 1992 when it was named Division Two. League One came into existence in 2004.

ALL THE WINNERS...

THIRD DIVISION

1921	Crystal Palace	

THIRD DIVISION NORTH/SOUTH

1922	Stockport County	Southampton
1923	Nelson	Bristol City
1924	Wolverhampton	Portsmouth
1925	Darlington	Swansea Town
1926	Grimsby Town	Reading
1927	Stoke City	Bristol City
1928	Bradford Park Avenue	Millwall
1929	Bradford City	Charlton Athletic
1930	Port Vale	Plymouth Argyle
1931	Chesterfield	Notts County
1932	Lincoln City	Fulham
1933	Hull City	Brentford
1934	Barnsley	Norwich City
1935	Doncaster Rovers	Charlton Athletic
1936	Chesterfield	Coventry City
1937	Stockport County	Luton Town
1938	Tranmere Rovers	Millwall
1939	Barnsley	Newport County
1939-46	World War II	
1947	Doncaster Rovers	Cardiff City
1948	Lincoln City	Queens Park Rangers
1949	Hull City	Swansea Town
1950	Doncaster Rovers	Notts County
1951	Rotherham United	Nottingham Forest

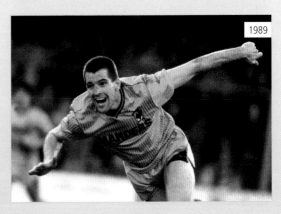

1989

1952	Lincoln City	Plymouth Argyle
1953	Oldham Athletic	Bristol Rovers
1954	Port Vale	Ipswich Town
1955	Barnsley	Bristol City
1956	Grimsby Town	Leyton Orient
1957	Derby County	Ipswich Town
1958	Scunthorpe United	Brighton and Hove Albion

THIRD DIVISION

1959	Plymouth Argyle
1960	Southampton
1961	Bury
1962	Portsmouth
1963	Northampton Town
1964	Coventry City
1965	Carlisle United
1966	Hull City
1967	Queens Park Rangers
1968	Oxford United
1969	Watford
1970	Leyton Orient
1971	Preston North End
1972	Aston Villa
1973	Bolton Wanderers
1974	Oldham Athletic
1975	Blackburn Rovers
1976	Hereford United
1977	Mansfield Town
1978	Wrexham
1979	Shrewsbury Town
1980	Grimsby Town
1981	Rotherham United
1982	Burnley
1983	Portsmouth
1984	Oxford United
1985	Bradford City
1986	Reading
1987	Bournemouth
1988	Sunderland

1989	Wolverhampton Wanderers
1990	Bristol Rovers
1991	Cambridge United
1992	Brentford

SECOND DIVISION

1993	Stoke City
1994	Reading
1995	Birmingham City
1996	Swindon Town
1997	Bury
1998	Watford
1999	Fulham
2000	Preston North End
2001	Millwall
2002	Brighton and Hove Albion
2003	Wigan Athletic
2004	Plymouth Argyle

2013

LEAGUE ONE

2005	Luton Town
2006	Southend United
2007	Scunthorpe United
2008	Swansea City
2009	Leicester City
2010	Norwich City
2011	Brighton and Hove Albion
2012	Charlton Athletic
2013	Doncaster Rovers

2012: Swindon boss Paolo Di Canio

LEAGUE TWO

League Two is the lowest tier of English professional football before the start of the non-league game.

From 1958 it was known as Division Four, following the decision to change the Third Divisions North and South into one league and create a new fourth level.

It became Division Three in 1992 and took up its current name in 2004.

2013

2008

1997

ALL THE WINNERS...

FOURTH DIVISION

1959 Port Vale
1960 Walsall
1961 Peterborough United
1962 Millwall
1963 Brentford
1964 Gillingham
1965 Brighton and Hove Albion
1966 Doncaster Rovers
1967 Stockport County
1968 Luton Town
1969 Doncaster Rovers
1970 Chesterfield
1971 Notts County
1972 Grimsby Town
1973 Southport
1974 Peterborough United
1975 Mansfield Town
1976 Lincoln City
1977 Cambridge United
1978 Watford
1979 Reading
1980 Huddersfield Town
1981 Southend United
1982 Sheffield United
1983 Wimbledon
1984 York City
1985 Chesterfield
1986 Swindon Town
1987 Northampton Town

1999

1988 Wolverhampton Wanderers
1989 Rotherham United
1990 Exeter City
1991 Darlington
1992 Burnley

2009

THIRD DIVISION

1993 Cardiff City
1994 Shrewsbury Town
1995 Carlisle United
1996 Preston North End
1997 Wigan Athletic
1998 Notts County
1999 Brentford
2000 Swansea City
2001 Brighton and Hove Albion
2002 Plymouth Argyle
2003 Rushden and Diamonds
2004 Doncaster Rovers

LEAGUE TWO

2005 Yeovil Town
2006 Carlisle United
2007 Walsall
2008 MK Dons
2009 Brentford
2010 Notts County
2011 Chesterfield
2012 Swindon Town
2013 Gillingham

SCOTLAND

The Scottish League was founded in 1890 and organised a second division in 1893.

A third division lasted just two seasons between 1923-25. From 1926-39 there were just two divisions. Three divisions began again in 1946 but went back to two in 1955. They were named Divisions 1 and 2 in 1956. In 1975 a third division was again back in operation.

In 1995 four divisions of ten teams came into operation before the breakaway Scottish Premier League came into existence in 1998.

SCOTTISH LEAGUE

1891	Dumbarton and Rangers
1892	Dumbarton
1893	Celtic

FIRST DIVISION

1894	Celtic
1895	Heart of Midlothian
1896	Celtic
1897	Heart of Midlothian
1898	Celtic
1899	Rangers
1900	Rangers
1901	Rangers
1902	Rangers
1903	Hibernian
1904	Third Lanark
1905	Celtic
1906	Celtic
1907	Celtic
1908	Celtic
1909	Celtic
1910	Celtic
1911	Rangers
1912	Rangers
1913	Rangers
1914	Celtic
1915	Celtic
1916	Celtic
1917	Celtic
1918	Rangers
1919	Celtic
1920	Rangers
1921	Rangers
1922	Celtic
1923	Rangers
1924	Rangers
1925	Rangers
1926	Celtic
1927	Rangers
1928	Rangers
1929	Rangers
1930	Rangers
1931	Rangers
1932	Motherwell
1933	Rangers
1934	Rangers
1935	Rangers
1936	Celtic
1937	Rangers
1938	Celtic
1939	Rangers
1939-46	World War II
1947	Rangers
1948	Hibernian
1949	Rangers
1950	Rangers
1951	Hibernian
1952	Hibernian
1953	Rangers
1954	Celtic
1955	Aberdeen
1956	Rangers
1957	Rangers
1958	Heart of Midlothian
1959	Rangers
1960	Heart of Midlothian
1961	Rangers
1962	Dundee
1963	Rangers
1964	Rangers
1965	Kilmarnock
1966	Celtic
1967	Celtic
1968	Celtic
1969	Celtic
1970	Celtic
1971	Celtic
1972	Celtic
1973	Celtic
1974	Celtic
1975	Rangers

PREMIER DIVISION

1976	Rangers
1977	Celtic
1978	Rangers
1979	Celtic
1980	Aberdeen
1981	Celtic
1982	Celtic
1983	Dundee United
1984	Aberdeen
1985	Aberdeen
1986	Celtic
1987	Rangers
1988	Celtic
1989	Rangers
1990	Rangers
1991	Rangers
1992	Rangers
1993	Rangers
1994	Rangers
1995	Rangers
1996	Rangers
1997	Rangers
1998	Celtic

PREMIER LEAGUE

1999	Rangers
2000	Rangers
2001	Celtic
2002	Celtic
2003	Rangers
2004	Celtic
2005	Rangers
2006	Celtic
2007	Celtic
2008	Celtic
2009	Rangers
2010	Rangers
2011	Rangers
2012	Celtic
2013	Celtic

DIVISION TWO

1894	Hibernian
1895	Hibernian
1896	Abercorn
1897	Partick Thistle
1898	Kilmarnock
1899	Kilmarnock
1900	Partick Thistle
1901	St. Bernard's
1902	Port Glasgow Athletic
1903	Airdrieonians
1904	Hamilton Academical
1905	Clyde
1906	Leith Athletic
1907	St. Bernard's
1908	Raith Rovers
1909	Abercorn
1910	Leith Athletic

2012: Celtic

1911	Dumbarton
1912	Ayr United
1913	Ayr United
1914	Cowdenbeath
1915	Cowdenbeath
1915-21	World War I
1922	Alloa Athletic
1923	Queen's Park
1924	St. Johnstone
1925	Dundee United
1926	Dunfermline Athletic
1927	Bo'ness United
1928	Ayr United
1929	Dundee United
1930	Leith Athletic
1931	Third Lanark
1932	East Stirlingshire
1933	Hibernian
1934	Albion Rovers
1935	Third Lanark
1936	Falkirk
1937	Ayr United
1938	Raith Rovers
1939	Cowdenbeath
1939-46	World War II

B DIVISION

1947	Dundee
1948	East Fife
1949	Raith Rovers
1950	Morton
1951	Queen of the South
1952	Clyde
1953	Stirling Albion
1954	Motherwell
1955	Airdrieonians
1956	Queen's Park

DIVISION TWO

1957	Clyde
1958	Stirling Albion
1959	Ayr United
1960	St. Johnstone
1961	Stirling Albion
1962	Clyde
1963	St. Johnstone
1964	Morton
1965	Stirling Albion
1966	Ayr United
1967	Morton
1968	St. Mirren
1969	Motherwell
1970	Falkirk
1971	Partick Thistle
1972	Dumbarton
1973	Clyde
1974	Airdrieonians
1975	Falkirk

2013

FIRST DIVISION

1976	Partick Thistle
1977	St. Mirren
1978	Morton
1979	Dundee
1980	Heart of Midlothian
1981	Hibernian
1982	Motherwell
1983	St. Johnstone
1984	Morton
1985	Motherwell
1986	Hamilton Academical
1987	Morton
1988	Hamilton Academical
1989	Dunfermline Athletic
1990	St. Johnstone
1991	Falkirk
1992	Dundee
1993	Raith Rovers
1994	Falkirk
1995	Raith Rovers
1996	Dunfermline Athletic
1997	St. Johnstone
1998	Dundee
1999	Hibernian
2000	St. Mirren
2001	Livingston
2002	Partick Thistle
2003	Falkirk
2004	Inverness Caledonian Thistle
2005	Falkirk
2006	St. Mirren
2007	Gretna
2008	Hamilton Academical
2009	St. Johnstone
2010	Inverness Caledonian Thistle
2011	Dunfermline Athletic
2012	Ross County
2013	Partick Thistle

DIVISION TWO

1999	Livingston
2000	Clyde
2001	Partick Thistle
2002	Queen of the South
2003	Raith Rovers
2004	Airdrie United
2005	Brechin City
2006	Gretna
2007	Greenock Morton
2008	Ross County
2009	Raith Rovers
2010	Stirling Albion
2011	Livingston
2012	Cowdenbeath
2013	Queen of the South

THIRD DIVISION

1924	Arthurlie
1925	Title not awarded as fixtures not completed

C DIVISION

1947	Stirling Albion
1948	East Stirlingshire
1949	Forfar Athletic
1949-55	Split into north-east and south-west sections
1950	Hibernian A Clyde A
1951	Heart of Midlothian A Clyde A
1952	Dundee A Rangers A
1953	Aberdeen A Rangers A
1954	Brechin City Rangers A
1955	Aberdeen A Partick Thistle A

DIVISION THREE

1995	Forfar Athletic
1996	Livingston
1997	Inverness Caledonian Thistle
1998	Alloa Athletic
1999	Ross County
2000	Queen's Park
2001	Hamilton Academical
2002	Brechin City
2003	Greenock Morton
2004	Stranraer
2005	Gretna
2006	Cowdenbeath
2007	Berwick Rangers
2008	East Fife
2009	Dumbarton
2010	Livingston
2011	Arbroath
2012	Alloa Athletic
2013	Rangers

THE FA CUP

1960

In season 2012-13 some 833 sides applied to enter the FA Cup and 758 were given the chance after meeting the competition's requirements. The final between Wigan Athletic and Manchester City attracted a crowd of 86,254 to the new Wembley Stadium.

An extra preliminary round for 400 teams began in August 2012 and there was another qualifying group before the first round proper when teams from League One and Two entered the competition.

The third round sees the entry of teams from the Premier League and Championship in the draw bag with games traditional played on the first Saturday in January.

After that round there are two more before the last eight reach the quarter-finals, then the semi-finals and final. Semis have been played in recent years at Wembley in order to give more fans the chance to get to see the games live.

The first final at Wembley was in 1923. Between 2001 and 2006 the final was staged at the Millennium Stadium in Cardiff but returned to Wembley in 2007, after the London stadium was rebuilt.

The world's oldest and most respected domestic knockout competition began with just 15 sides and a crowd of 2,000 attended the first final at Kennington Oval in South London.

1872 Wanderers 1 Royal Engineers 0
1873 Wanderers 2 Oxford University 0
1874 Oxford University 2 Royal Engineers 0
1875 Royal Engineers 1 Old Etonians 1
(replay Royal Engineers 2 Old Etonians 0)
1876 Wanderers 1 Old Etonians 1
(replay Wanderers 3 Old Etonians 0)
1877 Wanderers 2 Oxford University 1 aet
1878 Wanderers 3 Royal Engineers 1
1879 Old Etonians 1 Clapham Rovers 0
1880 Clapham Rovers 1 Oxford University 0
1881 Old Carthusians 3 Old Etonians 0
1882 Old Etonians 1 Blackburn Rovers 0
1883 Blackburn Olympic 2
Old Etonians 1 aet
1884 Blackburn Rovers 2
Queens Park, Glasgow 1
1885 Blackburn Rovers 2
Queens Park, Glasgow 0
1886 Blackburn Rovers 0
West Brom 0
(replay Blackburn 2 West Brom 0)
1887 Aston Villa 2
West Bromwich Albion 0

 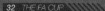

1888 West Brom 2 Preston North End 1

1889 Preston North End 3
Wolverhampton Wanderers 0

1890 Blackburn Rovers 6 The Wednesday 1

1891 Blackburn Rovers 3 Notts County 1

1892 West Bromwich Albion 3 Aston Villa 0

1893 Wolverhampton Wanderers 1 Everton 0

1894 Notts County 4 Bolton Wanderers 1

1895 Aston Villa 1 West Bromwich Albion 0

1896 The Wednesday 2
Wolverhampton Wanderers 1

1897 Aston Villa 3 Everton 2

1898 Nottingham Forest 3 Derby County 1

1899 Sheffield United 4 Derby County 1

1900 Bury 4 Southampton 0

1901 Tottenham Hotspur 2 Sheffield United 2
(replay Tottenham Hotspur 3 Sheffield United 1)

1902 Sheffield United 1 Southampton 1
(replay Sheffield United 2 Southampton 1)

1903 Bury 6 Derby County 0

1904 Manchester City 1 Bolton Wanderers 0

1905 Aston Villa 2 Newcastle United 0

1906 Everton 1 Newcastle United 0

1907 The Wednesday 2 Everton 1

1908 Wolverhampton Wanderers 3
Newcastle United 1

1909 Manchester United 1 Bristol City 0

1910 Newcastle United 1 Barnsley 1
(replay Newcastle United 2 Barnsley 0)

1911 Bradford City 0 Newcastle United 0
(replay Bradford City 1 Newcastle United 0)

1962

1966

1912 Barnsley 0 West Bromwich Albion 0
(replay Barnsley 1 West Bromwich Albion 0)

1913 Aston Villa 1 Sunderland 0

1914 Burnley 1 Liverpool 0

1915 Sheffield United 3 Chelsea 0

No competition due to First World War

1920 Aston Villa 1 Huddersfield Town 0 aet

1921 Tottenham Hotspur 1
Wolverhampton Wanderers 0

1922 Huddersfield Town 1 Preston North End 0

1923 Bolton Wanderers 2 West Ham United 0

1924 Newcastle United 2 Aston Villa 0

1925 Sheffield United 1 Cardiff City 0

1926 Bolton Wanderers 1 Manchester City 0

1927 Cardiff City 1 Arsenal 0

1928 Blackburn Rovers 3 Huddersfield Town 1

1929 Bolton Wanderers 2 Portsmouth 0

1930 Arsenal 2 Huddersfield Town 0

1931 West Bromwich Albion 2 Birmingham City 1

1932 Newcastle United 2 Arsenal 1

1933 Everton 3 Manchester City 0

1934 Manchester City 2 Portsmouth 1

1935 Sheffield Wednesday 4
West Bromwich Albion 2

1936 Arsenal 1 Sheffield United 0

1937 Sunderland 3 Preston North End 1

1938 Preston North End 1
Huddersfield Town 0 aet

1939 Portsmouth 4 Wolverhampton Wanderers 1

No competition due to Second World War

1946 Derby County 4 Charlton Athletic 1 aet

1972

1947 Charlton Athletic 1 Burnley 0 aet
1948 Manchester United 4 Blackpool 2
1949 Wolverhampton Wanderers 3
Leicester City 1
1950 Arsenal 2 Liverpool 0
1951 Newcastle United 2 Blackpool 0
1952 Newcastle United 1 Arsenal 0
1953 Blackpool 4 Bolton Wanderers 3
1954 West Bromwich Albion 3
Preston North End 2
1955 Newcastle United 3 Manchester City 1
1956 Manchester City 3 Birmingham City 1
1957 Aston Villa 2 Manchester United 1
1958 Bolton Wanderers 2 Manchester United 0
1959 Nottingham Forest 2 Luton Town 1
1960 Wolverhampton Wanderers 3
Blackburn Rovers 0
1961 Tottenham Hotspur 2 Leicester City 0
1962 Tottenham Hotspur 3 Burnley 1
1963 Manchester United 3 Leicester City 1
1964 West Ham United 3 Preston North End 2
1965 Liverpool 2 Leeds United 1 aet
1966 Everton 3 Sheffield Wednesday 2
1967 Tottenham Hotspur 2 Chelsea 1
1968 West Bromwich Albion 1 Everton 0 aet
1969 Manchester City 1 Leicester City 0

1970 Chelsea 2 Leeds United 2
(replay Chelsea 2 Leeds United 1)
1971 Arsenal 2 Liverpool 1 aet
1972 Leeds United 1 Arsenal 0
1973 Sunderland 1 Leeds United 0
1974 Liverpool 3 Newcastle United 0
1975 West Ham United 2 Fulham 0
1976 Southampton 1 Manchester United 0
1977 Manchester United 2 Liverpool 1
1978 Ipswich Town 1 Arsenal 0
1979 Arsenal 3 Manchester United 2
1980 West Ham United 1 Arsenal 0
1981 Tottenham Hotspur 1 Manchester City 1
(replay Tottenham Hotspur 3 Manchester City 2)
1982 Tottenham Hotspur 1
Queens Park Rangers 1
(replay Tottenham Hotspur 1 Queens Park Rangers 0)
1983 Manchester United 2
Brighton and Hove Albion 2
*(replay Manchester United 4
Brighton and Hove Albion 0)*
1984 Everton 2 Watford 0
1985 Manchester United 1 Everton 0 aet
1986 Liverpool 3 Everton 1
1987 Coventry City 3 Tottenham Hotspur 2 aet
1988 Wimbledon 1 Liverpool 0

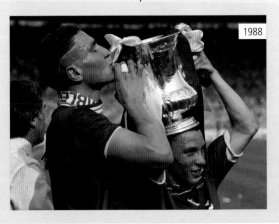

1988

1995

1989 Liverpool 3 Everton 2 aet
1990 Manchester United 3 Crystal Palace 3
(replay Manchester United 1 Crystal Palace 0)
1991 Tottenham Hotspur 2
Nottingham Forest 1 aet
1992 Liverpool 2 Sunderland 0
1993 Arsenal 1 Sheffield Wednesday 1
(replay Arsenal 2 Sheffield Wednesday 1 aet)
1994 Manchester United 4 Chelsea 0
1995 Everton 1 Manchester United 0

1996 Manchester United 1 Liverpool 0
1997 Chelsea 2 Middlesbrough 0
1998 Arsenal 2 Newcastle United 0
1999 Manchester United 2 Newcastle United 0
2000 Chelsea 1 Aston Villa 0
2001 Liverpool 2 Arsenal 1
2002 Arsenal 2 Chelsea 0
2003 Arsenal 1 Southampton 0
2004 Manchester United 3 Millwall 0
2005 Arsenal 0 Manchester United 0 aet
(Arsenal won 5-4 on penalties)
2006 Liverpool 3 West Ham United 3
(Liverpool won 3-1 on penalties)
2007 Chelsea 1 Manchester United 0 aet
2008 Portsmouth 1 Cardiff City 0
2009 Chelsea 2 Everton 1
2010 Chelsea 1 Portsmouth 0
2011 Manchester City 1 Stoke City 0
2012 Chelsea 2 Liverpool 1
2013 Wigan Athletic 1 Manchester City 0

2013

THE LEAGUE CUP

Swansea City became the first Welsh side to lift the League Cup when they beat Bradford City 5-0 in the 2013 final.

It was also the biggest margin of victory in the final since the cup began in 1960-61.

All 72 English Football League sides, plus the 20 teams in the Premier League, compete for the League Cup.

During its history sponsorship has seen it the called the Milk, Littlewoods, Rumbelows, Coca-Cola, Worthington, Carling and Capital One Cup.

For its first six years the final was a two-legged affair, played home and away. From 1967 onwards it has been a one-off final, played at Wembley when the stadium has been available.

1976

2001

2008

2012

1987

ALL THE WINNERS...

1961 Aston Villa (0) 3 Rotherham (2) 0 aet
1962 Norwich (3) 1 Rochdale (0) 0
1963 Birmingham City (3) 0 Aston Villa (1) 0
1964 Leicester (1) 3 Stoke City (1) 2
1965 Chelsea (3) 0 Leicester (2) 0
1966 West Brom (1) 4 West Ham (2) 1
1967 QPR 3 West Brom 2
1968 Leeds 1 Arsenal 0
1969 Swindon 3 Arsenal 1 aet
1970 Manchester City 2 West Brom 1 aet
1971 Tottenham 2 Aston Villa 0
1972 Stoke City 2 Chelsea 1
1973 Tottenham 1 Norwich City 0
1974 Wolves 2 Manchester City 1
1975 Aston Villa 1 Norwich 0
1976 Manchester City 2 Newcastle 1
1977 Aston Villa 3 Everton 2
*(second replay Old Trafford, 0-0 Wembley,
1-1 Hillsborough aet)*
1978 Nottingham Forest 1 Liverpool 0
(replay Old Trafford, 0-0 Wembley)
1979 Nottingham Forest 3 Southampton 2
1980 Wolves 1 Nottingham Forest 0
1981 Liverpool 2 West Ham 1
(replay Villa Park, 1-1 Wembley)
1982 Liverpool 3 Tottenham 1 aet
1983 Liverpool 2 Manchester United 1 aet
1984 Liverpool 1 Everton 0
(replay Maine Road, 0-0 Wembley)
1985 Norwich 1 Sunderland 0
1986 Oxford United 3 QPR 0
1987 Arsenal 2 Liverpool 1
1988 Luton Town 3 Arsenal 2
1989 Nottingham Forest 3 Luton Town 1
1990 Nottingham Forest 1 Oldham 0
1991 Sheffield Wednesday 1 Manchester United 0
1992 Manchester United 1 Nottingham Forest 0
1993 Arsenal 2 Sheffield Wednesday 1

1994 Aston Villa 3 Manchester United 1
1995 Liverpool 2 Bolton 1
1996 Aston Villa 3 Leeds 0
1997 Leicester 1 Middlesbrough 0
(replay at Hillsborough, 1-1 at Wembley)
1998 Chelsea 2 Middlesbrough 0 aet
1999 Tottenham 1 Leicester 0
2000 Leicester 2 Tranmere 1
2001 Liverpool 1 Birmingham 1
(Liverpool 5-4, penalty shoot-out)
2002 Blackburn 2 Tottenham 1
2003 Liverpool 2 Manchester United 0
2004 Middlesbrough 2 Bolton 1
2005 Chelsea 3 Liverpool 2 aet
2006 Manchester United 4 Wigan 0
2007 Chelsea 2 Arsenal 1
2008 Tottenham 2 Chelsea 1 aet
2009 Manchester United 0 Tottenham 0
(United 4-1, penalty shoot-out)
2010 Manchester United 2 Aston Villa 1
2011 Birmingham City 2 Arsenal 1
2012 Liverpool 2 Cardiff City 2
(Liverpool 3-2, penalty shoot-out)
2013 Swansea City 5 Bradford City 0

2013

EUROPEAN CUP

CHAMPIONS LEAGUE

Although it's had a few name changes over the years, Europe's biggest club competition is still played for the European Cup.

It began life in 1955-56 as the European Champion Clubs' Cup, which then became known as the European Cup. The competition became the Champions League in 1992.

Originally played on a knockout basis, the competition now involves a group/league stage format before knockout rounds.

Real Madrid, who won the trophy during the event's first five years of existence, are the most successful side in the even with nine titles to their credit.

ALL THE WINNERS...

1956 Real Madrid 4 Stade de Reims 3
1957 Real Madrid 2 Fiorentina 0
1958 Real Madrid 3 AC Milan 2 aet
1959 Real Madrid 2 Stade de Reims 0
1960 Real Madrid 7 Eintracht Frankfurt 3
1961 Benfica 3 Barcelona 2
1962 Benfica 5 Real Madrid 3
1963 AC Milan 2 Benfica 1
1964 Inter Milan 3 Real Madrid 1

1979

1965 Inter Milan 1 Benfica 0
1966 Real Madrid 2 Partizan 1
1967 Celtic 2 Inter Milan 1
1968 Manchester United 4 Benfica 1 aet
1969 AC Milan 4 Ajax 1
1970 Feyenoord 2 Celtic 1 aet
1971 Ajax 2 Panathinaikos 0
1972 Ajax 2 Inter Milan 0
1973 Ajax 1 Juventus 0
1974 Bayern Munich 4 Atletico Madrid 0
(replay, first game 1-1)

1997

2002

2007

1975 Bayern Munich 2 Leeds United 0

1976 Bayern Munich 1 Saint Etienne 0

1977 Liverpool 3
Borussia Monchengladbach 1

1978 Liverpool 1 Club Brugge 0

1979 Nottingham Forest 1 Malmo 0

1980 Nottingham Forest 1 Hamburg 0

1981 Liverpool 1 Real Madrid 0

1982 Aston Villa 1 Bayern Munich 0

1983 Hamburg 1 Juventus 0

1984 Liverpool 1 Roma 1
(Liverpool 4-2 on penalties)

1985 Juventus 1 Liverpool 0

1986 Steaua Bucharest 0 Barcelona 0
(Bucharest 2-0 on penalties)

1987 Porto 2 Bayern Munich 1

1988 PSV Eindhoven 0 Benfica 0
(PSV 6-5 on penalties)

1989 AC Milan 4 Steaua Bucharest 0

1990 AC Milan 1 Benfica 0

1991 Red Star Belgrade 0 Marseille 0
(Red Star 5-3 on penalties)

1992 Barcelona 1 Sampdoria 0 aet

1993 Marseille 1 AC Milan 0

1994 AC Milan 4 Barcelona 0

1995 Ajax 1 AC Milan 0

1996 Juventus 1 Ajax 1
(Juventus 4-2 on penalties)

1997 Borussia Dortmund 3 Juventus 1

1998 Real Madrid 1 Juventus 0

1999 Manchester United 2 Bayern Munich 1

2000 Real Madrid 3 Valencia 0

2001 Bayern Munich 1 Valencia 1
(Bayern 5-4 on penalties)

2002 Real Madrid 2 Bayer Leverkusen 1

2003 AC Milan 0 Juventus 0
(Milan 3-2 on penalties)

2004 Porto 3 Monaco 0

2005 Liverpool 3 AC Milan 3
(Liverpool 3-2 on penalties)

2006 Barcelona 2 Arsenal 1

2007 AC Milan 2 Liverpool 1

2008 Manchester United 1 Chelsea 1
(United 6-5 on penalties)

2009 Barcelona 2 Manchester United 0

2010 Inter Milan 2 Bayern Munich 0

2011 Barcelona 3 Manchester United 1

2012 Bayern Munich 1 Chelsea 1
(Chelsea 4-3 on penalties)

2013 Bayern Munich 2 Borussia Dortmund 1

2013

EUROPA LEAGUE
UEFA CUP/INTER CITIES FAIRS CUP

Initially the Inter-Cities Fairs Cup, from 1958-71, the event was then taken over by UEFA, European football's governing body, to become the UEFA Cup.

The UEFA Cup ran until 2010 when it became known as the Europa League and changed its format.

It is the secondary competition to the European Champions League. Teams qualify for the tournament subject to where they finish in their leagues, or by winning certain domestic cups – plus some teams that are eliminated from the Champions League.

The former Cup Winners' Cup ran until 1999 and the InterToto Cup to 2009 before being absorbed into this competition.

INTER CITIES FAIRS CUP

(Two leg scores in brackets)

1958 London 2 Barcelona 8 (2-2, 6-0)*
1960 Birmingham 1 Barcelona 4 (0-0, 4-1) **
1961 Birmingham 2 Roma 4 (2-2, 2-0)
1962 Valencia 7 Barcelona 3 (6-2, 1-1)
1963 Dynamo Zagreb 1 Valencia 4 (1-2, 2-0)
1964 Real Zaragoza 2 Valencia 1
1965 Ferencvaros 1 Juventus 0
1966 Barcelona 4 Zaragoza 3 (0-1, 2-4)

1970

1967 Dynamo Zagreb 2 Leeds 0 (2-0, 0-0)
1968 Leeds United 1 Ferencvaros 0 (1-0, 0-0)
1969 Newcastle United 6 U. Dozsa 2 (3-0, 2-3)
1970 Arsenal 4 Anderlect 3 (3-1, 3-0)
1971 Leeds United 3 Juventus 3
(2-2, 1-1, Leeds won on away goals)
Ran between 1955-58.
**Ran between 1959-60*

1974

UEFA CUP

1972 Tottenham 3 Wolves 2 (1-2, 1-1)
1973 Liverpool 3 B. Monchengladbach 2 (3-0, 2-0)
1974 Feyenoord 4 Tottenham 2 (2-2, 2-0)
1975 B. Monchengladbach 5 Twente 1 (0-0, 1-5)
1976 Liverpool 4 Brugge 3 (2-2, 1-1)
1977 Juventus 2 Athletic Bilbao 2 (1-0. 2-1, Juventus away goal)
1978 PSV Eindhoven 3 v Bastia 0 (0-0, 3-0)
1979 B. Monchengladbach 2 Red Star 1 (1-1, 1-0)
1980 E. Frankfurt 3 B. Monchengladbach 3 (2-1, 1-1, Eintracht away goal)
1981 Ipswich Town 5 v Alkmaar 4 (3-0, 4-2)
1982 IFK Gothenburg 4 Hamburg 0 (1-0, 0-3
1983 Anderlecht 2 Benfica 1 (1-0, 1-1)
1984 Tottenham 2 Anderlecht 2 (1-1, 1-1)
(2-2, aet, Spurs 4-3 pens)
1985 Real Madrid 3 Videotron 1 (0-3, 0-1)
1986 Real Madrid 5 Cologne 3 (5-1, 2-0)
1987 IFK Gothenburg 2 Dundee United 1 (1-0, 1-1)
1988 B. Leverkusen 3 Espanyol 3 (3-0, 3-0)

(3-3, aet, Bayer 3-2 pens)
1989 Napoli 5 Stuttgart 4 (2-1, 3-3)
1990 Juventus 3 Fiorentina 1 (3-1, 0-0)
1991 Inter Milan 2 Roma 1 (2-0, 1-0)
1992 Ajax 2 Torino 2 (2-2, 0-0, away goal)
1993 Juventus 6 B. Dortmund 1 (1-3, 3-0)
1994 Inter Milan 3 Salzburg 0 (0-1, 1-0)
1995 Parma 2 Juventus 1 (1-0, 1-1)
1996 B. Munich 5 Bordeaux 1 (2-0, 1-3)
1997 Schalke 04 1 Inter Milan 1 (1-0, 1-0,
1-1, aet, Schalke 4-1 pens)
1998 Inter Milan 3 Lazio 0
1999 Parma 3 Marseille 0
2000 Galatasaray 0 Arsenal 0 (Gala 4-1 pens)
2001 Liverpool 5 Alaves 4 (aet, sudden death)
2002 Feyenoord 3 Borussia Dortmund 2
2003 Porto 3 Celtic 2 (aet)
2004 Valencia 2 Marseille 0
2005 CSKA Moscow 3 Sporting Lisbon 1
2006 Sevilla 4 Middlesbrough 0
2007 Sevilla 2 Espanyol 2 (aet, Sevilla 3-1 pens)
2008 Zenit St. Petersburg 2 Rangers 0
2009 Shakhtar Donetsk 2 Werder Bremen 1 aet

EUROPA LEAGUE
2010 Atletico Madrid 2 Fulham 1 (aet)
2011 Porto 1 Braga 0
2012 Atletico Madrid 3 Athletic Bilbao 0
2013 Benfica 1 Chelsea 2

2013

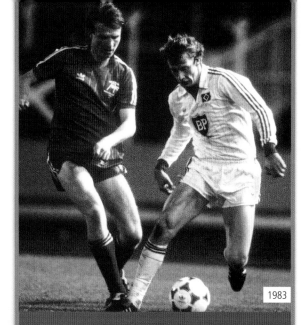
1983

UEFA SUPER CUP

The winners of the Champions League and the Europa League meet in the European Super Cup. Now a one-off game, it was a two-legged event from 1972-1997 and a single tie in 1984, 1986 and 1991. It was not staged in 1974, 1981, 1985.

1972 Ajax	**1993** Parma
1973 Ajax	**1994** AC Milan
1974 Not played	**1995** Ajax
1975 Dynamo Kiev	**1996** Juventus
1976 Anderlecht	**1997** Barcelona
1977 Liverpool	**1998** Chelsea
1978 Anderlecht	**1999** Lazio
1979 Nottingham	**2001** Liverpool
Forest	**2002** Real Madrid
1980 Valencia	**2003** AC Milan
1981 Not played	**2004** Valencia
1982 Aston Villa	**2005** Liverpool
1983 Aberdeen	**2006** Sevilla
1984 Juventus	**2007** AC Milan
1985 Not played	**2008** Zenit St.
1986 Steaua Bucharest	Petersburg
1987 Porto	**2009** Barcelona
1988 Mechelen	**2010** Atletico Madrid
1989 AC Milan	**2011** Barcelona
1990 AC Milan	**2012** Atletico Madrid
1991 Man United	
1992 Barcelona	

CHAMPIONS:
FRANCE

France's first professional league, the National, ran in 1932-33 and then became Division One. In 2002 it took on its current title of Ligue 1. Marseille and Saint-Etienne are the most successful sides.

1985

ALL THE WINNERS...

1933	Olympique Lillois	**1966**	Nantes	**1994**	Paris Saint German
1934	Sete	**1967**	Saint-Etienne	**1995**	Nantes
1935	Sochaux	**1968**	Saint-Etienne	**1996**	Auxerre
1936	RCF Paris	**1969**	Saint-Etienne	**1997**	Monaco
1937	Marseille	**1970**	Saint-Etienne	**1998**	Lens
1938	Sochaux	**1971**	Marseille	**1999**	Bordeaux
1939	Sete	**1972**	Marseille	**2000**	Monaco
1940-45	World War II	**1973**	Nantes	**2001**	Nantes
1946	Lille	**1974**	Saint-Etienne	**2002**	Lyon
1947	Roubaix-Tourcoing	**1975**	Saint-Etienne	**2003**	Lyon
1948	Marseille	**1976**	Saint-Etienne	**2004**	Lyon
1949	Stade Reims	**1977**	Nantes	**2005**	Lyon
1950	Bordeaux	**1978**	Monaco	**2006**	Lyon
1951	Nice	**1979**	Strasbourg	**2007**	Lyon
1952	Nice	**1980**	Nantes	**2008**	Lyon
1953	Stade Reims	**1981**	Saint-Etienne	**2009**	Bordeaux
1954	Lille	**1982**	Monaco	**2010**	Marseille
1955	Stade Reims	**1983**	Nantes	**2011**	Lille
1956	Nice	**1984**	Bordeaux	**2012**	Montpellier
1957	Saint-Etienne	**1985**	Bordeaux	**2013**	Paris Saint-Germain
1958	Stade Reims	**1986**	Paris Saint German	*Stripped of title*	
1959	Nice	**1987**	Bordeaux		
1960	Stade Reims	**1988**	Monaco		
1961	Monaco	**1989**	Marseille		
1962	Stade Reims	**1990**	Marseille		
1963	Monaco	**1991**	Marseille		
1964	Saint-Etienne	**1992**	Marseille		
1965	Nantes	**1993**	Marseille*		

2013

CHAMPIONS:
GERMANY

The Bundesliga was only formed in 1963. There are now second and third divisions in Germany. Bayern Munich are the most successful side.

ALL THE WINNERS...

2013

1964 Cologne
1965 Werder Bremen
1966 Munich 1860
1967 Eintracht Braunschweig
1968 Nuremberg
1969 Bayern Munich
1970 Borussia Monchengladbach
1971 Borussia Monchengladbach
1972 Bayern Munich
1973 Bayern Munich
1974 Bayern Munich
1975 Borussia Monchengladbach
1976 Borussia Monchengladbach
1977 Borussia Monchengladbach
1978 Cologne
1979 Hamburg
1980 Bayern Munich
1981 Bayern Munich
1982 Hamburg
1983 Hamburg
1984 Stuttgart
1985 Bayern Munich
1986 Bayern Munich

1987 Bayern Munich
1988 Werder Bremen
1989 Bayern Munich
1990 Bayern Munich
1991 Kaiserslautern
1992 Stuttgart
1993 Werder Bremen
1994 Bayern Munich
1995 Borussia Dortmund
1996 Borussia Dortmund
1997 Bayern Munich
1998 Kaiserslautern
1999 Bayern Munich
2000 Bayern Munich
2001 Bayern Munich
2002 Borussia Dortmund
2003 Bayern Munich
2004 Werder Bremen
2005 Bayern Munich
2006 Bayern Munich
2007 Stuttgart
2008 Bayern Munich
2009 Wolfsburg
2010 Bayern Munich
2011 Borussia Dortmund
2012 Borussia Dortmund
2013 Bayern Munich

1979

CHAMPIONS:
HOLLAND

Holland's Eredivisie began in 1956 and there is also a second division known as the Eerste Divisie. Amsterdam's Ajax are the most successful side.

ALL THE WINNERS...

2007

1957	Ajax	**1973**	Ajax
1958	DOS	**1974**	Feyenoord
1959	Sparta	**1975**	PSV Eindhoven
1960	Ajax	**1976**	PSV Eindhoven
1961	Feyenoord	**1977**	Ajax
1962	Feyenoord	**1978**	PSV Eindhoven
1963	PSV Eindhoven	**1979**	Ajax
1964	DWS	**1980**	Ajax
1965	Feyenoord	**1981**	AZ 67
1966	Ajax	**1982**	Ajax
1967	Ajax	**1983**	Ajax
1968	Ajax	**1984**	Feyenoord
1969	Feyenoord	**1985**	Ajax
1970	Ajax	**1986**	PSV Eindhoven
1971	Feyenoord	**1987**	PSV Eindhoven
1972	Ajax	**1988**	PSV Eindhoven

1996

1989	PSV Eindhoven
1990	Ajax
1991	PSV Eindhoven
1992	PSV Eindhoven
1993	Feyenoord
1994	Ajax
1995	Ajax
1996	Ajax
1997	PSV Eindhoven
1998	Ajax
1999	Feyenoord
2000	PSV Eindhoven
2001	PSV Eindhoven
2002	Ajax
2003	PSV Eindhoven
2004	Ajax
2005	PSV Eindhoven
2006	PSV Eindhoven
2007	PSV Eindhoven
2008	PSV Eindhoven
2009	AZ
2010	Twente
2011	Ajax
2012	Ajax
2013	Ajax

CHAMPIONS:
ITALY

Serie A is Italy's highest division. It was founded in 1898 as a divisional contest before becoming a single league in 1929. Juventus are the most successful side.

PRIMA CATEGORIA

1898	Genoa
1899	Genoa
1900	Genoa
1901	AC Milan
1902	Genoa
1903	Genoa
1904	Genoa
1905	Juventus
1906	AC Milan
1907	AC Milan
1908	Pro Vercelli
1909	Pro Vercelli
1910	Inter Milan
1911	Pro Vercelli
1912	Pro Vercelli
1913	Pro Vercelli
1914	Casale
1915	Genoa
1916-19	World War I
1920	Inter Milan
1921	Pro Vercelli
1922	Novese

PRIMA DIVISIONE

1922	Pro Vercelli
1923	Genoa
1924	Genoa
1925	Bologna
1926	Juventus

DIVISIONE NAZIONALE

1927	Torino*
1928	Torino
1929	Bologna

SERIE A

1930	Inter Milan
1931	Juventus
1932	Juventus
1933	Juventus
1934	Juventus
1935	Juventus
1936	Bologna
1937	Bologna
1938	Inter Milan
1939	Bologna
1940	Inter Milan
1941	Bologna
1942	Roma
1943	Torino
1944-45	World War II
1946	Torino
1947	Torino
1948	Torino
1949	Torino
1950	Juventus
1951	AC Milan
1952	Juventus
1953	Inter Milan
1954	Inter Milan
1955	AC Milan
1956	Fiorentina
1957	AC Milan
1958	Juventus
1959	AC Milan
1960	Juventus
1961	Juventus
1962	AC Milan
1963	Inter Milan
1964	Bologna
1965	Inter Milan
1966	Inter Milan
1967	Juventus
1968	AC Milan
1969	Fiorentina
1970	Cagliari Calcio
1971	Inter Milan
1972	Juventus
1973	Juventus
1974	Lazio
1975	Juventus
1976	Torino
1977	Juventus
1978	Juventus
1979	AC Milan
1980	Inter Milan
1981	Juventus
1982	Juventus
1983	Romas
1984	Juventus
1985	Verona
1986	Juventus
1987	Napoli
1988	AC Milan
1989	Inter Milan
1990	Napoli
1991	Sampdoria
1992	AC Milan
1993	AC Milan
1994	AC Milan
1995	Juventus
1996	AC Milan
1997	Juventus
1998	Juventus
1999	AC Milan
2000	Lazio
2001	Roma
2002	Juventus
2003	Juventus
2004	AC Milan
2005	Juventus*
2006	Inter Milan
2007	Inter Milan
2008	Inter Milan
2009	Inter Milan
2010	Inter Milan
2011	AC Milan
2012	Juventus
2013	Juventus

Stripped of title

CHAMPIONS: SPAIN

La Liga is Spain's top division and was founded in 1929. Real Madrid are the most successful side.

2013

ALL THE WINNERS...

1929	Barcelona		**1957**	Real Madrid
1930	Athletic Bilbao		**1958**	Real Madrid
1931	Athletic Bilbao		**1959**	Barcelona
1932	Real Madrid		**1960**	Barcelona
1933	Real Madrid		**1961**	Real Madrid
1934	Athletic Bilbao		**1962**	Real Madrid
1935	Real Betis		**1963**	Real Madrid
1936	Athletic Bilbao		**1964**	Real Madrid
1936-39	Spanish Civil War		**1965**	Real Madrid
1940	Atletico Aviacion		**1966**	Atletico Madrid
1941	Atletico Aviacion		**1967**	Real Madrid
1942	Valencia		**1968**	Real Madrid
1943	Athletic Bilbao			
1944	Valencia			
1945	Barcelona			
1946	Sevilla			
1947	Valencia			
1948	Barcelona			
1949	Barcelona			

1974

1954

1950	Atletico Madrid		**1969**	Real Madrid		**1982**	Real Sociedad
1951	Atletico Madrid		**1970**	Atletico Madrid		**1983**	Athletic Bilbao
1952	Barcelona		**1971**	Valencia		**1984**	Athletic Bilbao
1953	Barcelona		**1972**	Real Madrid		**1985**	Barcelona
1954	Real Madrid		**1973**	Atletico Madrid		**1986**	Real Madrid
1955	Real Madrid		**1974**	Barcelona		**1987**	Real Madrid
1956	Athletic Bilbao		**1975**	Real Madrid		**1988**	Real Madrid
			1976	Real Madrid		**1989**	Real Madrid
			1977	Atletico Madrid		**1990**	Real Madrid
			1978	Real Madrid		**1991**	Barcelona
			1979	Real Madrid		**1992**	Barcelona
			1980	Real Madrid		**1993**	Barcelona
			1981	Real Sociedad		**1994**	Barcelona
						1995	Real Madrd
						1996	Atletico Madrid
						1997	Real Madrid
						1998	Barcelona
						1999	Barcelona
						2000	Deportivo La Coruna
						2001	Real Madrid
						2002	Valencia
						2003	Real Madrid
						2004	Valencia
						2005	Barcelona
						2006	Barcelona
						2007	Real Madrid
						2008	Real Madrid
						2009	Barcelona
						2010	Barcelona
						2011	Barcelona
						2012	Real Madrid
						2013	Barcelona

CHAMPIONS:
EUROPES OTHER MAJOR LEAGUES

BULGARIA
League: A PFG
Founded: 1924
2012-13 Champions:
Ludogorets Razgrad

CROATIA
League:
Prva HNL
Founded: 1992
2012-13 Champions:
Dinamo Zagreb

CZECH REPUBLIC
League:
Gambrinus Liga
Founded: 1993
2012-13 Champions:
Viktoria Plzen

DENMARK
League:
Superliga
Founded: 1991
2012-13 Champions:
FC Copenhagen

FINLAND
League:
Veikkausliiga
Founded: 1990
2011-12 Champions:
HJK Helsinki

GREECE
League:
Superleague
Founded: 1927 (2006)
2012-13 Champions:
Olympiacos

ISRAEL
League:
Premier
Founded: 1999
2012-13 Champions:
Maccabi Tel Aviv

NORWAY
League:
Tippeligaen
Founded: 1937 (1991)
2012 Champions:
Molde

POLAND
League:
Ekstraklasa
Founded: 1927
2012-13 Champions:
Legia Warsaw

PORTUGAL
League:
Primeira
Founded: 1934
2012-13 Champions:
Porto

ROMANIA
League: Liga 1
Founded: 1909
2012-13 Champions:
Steaua Bucharest

RUSSIA
League: Premier
Founded: 2001
2012-13 Champions:
CSKA Moscow

SERBIA
League:
SuperLiga
Founded: 1923 (2006)
2012-13 Champions:
Partizan Belgrade
SLOVAKIA

League: Corgon Liga
Founded: 1993
2012-13 Champions:
Slovan Bratislava

SWEDEN

League:
Allsvenskan
Founded: 1924
2012 Champions:
Elfsborg

SWIZERLAND

League: Super League
Founded: 1897 (2003)
2012-13 Champions:
Basel

TURKEY
League:
Super Lig
Founded: 1959
2012-13 Champions:
Galatasaray

UKRAINE
League: Premier
Founded: 1991
2012-13 Champions:
Shakhtar Donetsk

CHAMPIONS OF THE WORLD

There is football life outside of the major European leagues!
Here are some winners from other continents.

Thierry Henry, New York Red Bulls

NORTH AMERICA

The MLS (Major League Soccer) got a massive boost when the likes of David Beckham and Robbie Keane (both LA Galaxy) and Thierry Henry (New York Red Bulls) and other stars from Europe agreed to play for teams in the competition.

Formed in 1993, the season runs from March to December, and involves 16 teams from the US and three from Canada in the Eastern and Western Conference.

The top five clubs in each Conference reach the play-offs where they go for the MLS Cup.

2012 Champions: LA Galaxy
Most titles: LA Galazy and DC United, both 4

David Beckham, formerly LA Galaxy

Carlos Tevez, formerly Boca Juniors

SOUTH AMERICA

The two major leagues are in Argentina (Primera Division) and Brazil (Serie A).

The Argentine division has 20 clubs and plays from August to May. Each season is divided into two tournaments, the Inicial and Final. The winners of these tournaments play a final game to decide the champions.

Among the competition's most famous clubs are Boca Juniors, who included Walter Samuel and Pablo Ledesma in their ranks; River Plate, whose former players include Javier Mascherano, Gonzalo Higuain and Radamel Falcao; Independiente and Racing.

2012 Champions: Velez Sarsfield
Most titles: River Plate, 34

In Brazil, Serie A or the Brasileirão, is also competed for by 20 clubs and runs from May to December.

Brazil football used to rely heavily on its state competitions and didn't really have a national champion until 1959. Among the famous clubs are Santos, the home of Pele; Palmeiras, Sao Paulo, Flamengo and Corinthians, where Manchester City striker Carlos Tevez and Arsenal defender Andre Santos both played.

2012 Champions: Fluminese
Most titles: Santos, Palmeiras, both 8

SOUTH AFRICA

The ABSA Premiership began in 1996 and 16 teams compete from August to May. Kaizer Chiefs are noted for former players Shaun Bartlett (Charlton) and Lucas Radebe (Leeds United), who both played in the English Premier League.

2013 Champions: Kaizer Chiefs
Most titles: Mamelodi Sundowns, 5

Shaun Bartlett at Charlton

AUSTRALIA

The A-League began in 2005 and consists of nine teams from Australia and one from New Zealand. Former Sheffield United defender Nick Montgomery was in the Central Coast Mariners squad that won the 2012-13 title. Sydney FC included ex-Blackburn midfielder Brett Emerton and legendary Italy striker Alessandro Del Piero

2013 Champions: Central Coast Mariners
Most titles: Brisbane Roar, Melbourne Victory, Sydney FC, all 2

Alessandro Del Piero, Sydney FC

The Ton-Up Club

ENGLAND

Steven Gerrard and Ashley Cole are the two latest players to reach the 100 appearances for England mark. Here are all seven Three Lions stars to hit that amazing total…

125

Peter Shilton

England: 1970-90
Debut age: 20
Clubs whilst international:
Leicester City, Stoke City, Nottingham Forest, Southampton, Derby County

The man who took over between the sticks from England's World Cup-winning keeper Gordon Banks. Shilts didn't have things all his own way though as he always had Liverpool and Tottenham shot-stopper Ray Clemence breathing down his neck. The fact that Clem won 61caps during Shilton's time in a Three Lions shirt shows just how strong competition was for the No.1 shirt at the time.

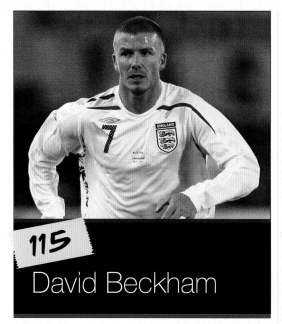

115
David Beckham

England: 1996-09
Debut age: 21
Clubs whilst international: Man United, Real Madrid, LA Galaxy, AC Milan
Although he never gave up hope of winning another England cap, now that Beckham has finally announced his retirement from the game he will not add to his already impressive total. The midfielder's set pieces raised his profile but his ball distribution, long passes and his battling qualities made him a first pick for more than 13 years.

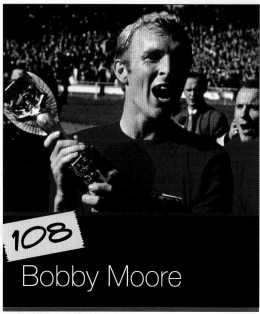

108
Bobby Moore

England: 1962-73
Debut age: 21
Clubs whilst International: West Ham
One of the most cultured defenders ever to grace the game, Essex-born Moore captained England to their World Cup victory in 1966. A cool customer on the ball who made the game look so very simple, he even earned praise from the great Pele. And that isn't won easily! Captained England 90 times. Passed away in 1993 at the age of just 51.

106
Bobby Charlton

England: 1958-70
Debut age: 20
Clubs whilst International: Man United
England's record goal scorer with 49 despite the fact he was not regarded as an out and out striker. The Geordie also hit 249 goals during an incredible 758 games for Manchester United, a record until beaten in 2008 by Ryan Giggs. Charlton, now 75 and a United director, was also part of the 1966 World Cup side.

105
Billy Wright

England: 1946-59
Debut age: 21
Clubs whilst International: Wolves
The central defender was the first player in the world to record 100 appearances for his country and also captained England on 90 occasions, the same as Moore. Shropshire-born Wright made his first appearance the month before his 22nd birthday and at one stage played 70 consecutive games. Passed away in 1994 at the age of 70.

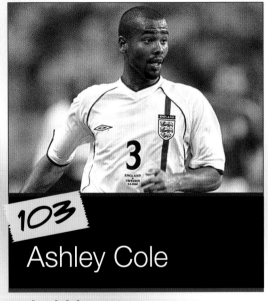

103
Ashley Cole

England debut: 2001
Debut age: 20
Clubs whilst International: Arsenal, Chelsea
His century of caps came in February's friendly victory over Brazil. Not his best game by a long way but still a milestone for a player whose contributions are not always appreciated by fans, despite being acknowledged by many as one of the best left backs in the world.

* All international appearances correct as of July 1, 2013.

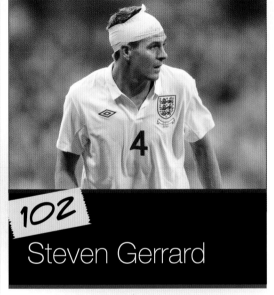

102
Steven Gerrard

England debut: 2000
Debut age: 20
Clubs whilst International: Liverpool
Made his debut the day after his 20th birthday in 2000. Scored his first goal in the celebrated 5-1 World Cup qualifying victory in Germany in September 2001. Missed the 2002 World Cup due to injury but appeared at the finals in 2006 and 2010. Was captain for the latter tournament and was handed the skipper's armband by current boss Roy Hodgson in 2012, when he led the side at the European Championships.

BUBBLING UNDER

Just two players in the current Three Lions set-up are currently anywhere near hitting the 100-cap mark for their country:

97
Frank Lampard

England debut: 1999
Debut age: 21
Clubs whilst international:
West Ham, Chelsea
With his future at Chelsea now looking safe until 2014, it's a good bet that midfielder Lamps will hit the ton. There won't be a problem selecting him if he is playing top-flight football – and the midfielder has proved that he is still one of the fittest players in the Premier League.

83
Wayne Rooney

England debut: 2003
Debut age: 17
Clubs whilst international:
Everton, Man United
The Manchester United striker – who has added a whole lot more to his game with his ability to play in midfield and drop back to defend – might have hit the 100-mark by now if it hadn't been for injuries and suspensions. With his 28th birthday in October 2013 he's arguably at his peak, so adding more games to his total should not be a problem. England's youngest player until the record was beaten by Theo Walcott.

Now turn the page to discover the full list of players who had made 50 or more appearances for England

50 or more appearances for England

ENGLAND

125 PETER SHILTON, Keeper, 1970-90

115 DAVID BECKHAM, Midfielder, 1996-09

108 BOBBY MOORE, Defender, 1962-73

106 BOBBY CHARLTON, Forward, 1958-70

105 BILLY WRIGHT, Defender, 1946-59

103 ASHLEY COLE, Defender, 2001-

102 STEVEN GERRARD, Midfielder, 2000-

97 FRANK LAMPARD, Midfielder, 1999-

90 BRYAN ROBSON, Midfielder, 1980-91

89 MICHAEL OWEN, Striker, 1998-08

86 KENNY SANSOM, Defender, 1979-88

85 GARY NEVILLE, Defender, 1995-07

84 RAY WILKINS, Midfielder, 1976-86

81 RIO FERDINAND, Defender, 1997-13

80 GARY LINEKER, Striker, 1984-92

79 WAYNE ROONEY, Striker, 2003-

79 JOHN BARNES, Midfielder, 1983-95

78 STUART PEARCE, Defender, 1987-99

78 JOHN TERRY, Defender, 2003-12

77 TERRY BUTCHER, Defender, 1980-90

76 TOM FINNEY, Forward, 1946-58

75 DAVID SEAMAN, Keeper, 1988-02

73 GORDON BANKS, Keeper, 1963-72

73 SOL CAMPBELL, Defender, 1996-07

72 ALAN BALL, Midfielder, 1965-75

67 MARTIN PETERS, Midfielder, 1966-74

66 TONY ADAMS, Defender, 1987-00

66 PAUL SCHOLES, Midfielder, 1997-04

65 DAVE WATSON, Defender, 1974-82

63 RAY WILSON, Defender, 1960-68

63 KEVIN KEEGAN, Forward, 1972-82

63 ALAN SHEARER, Striker, 1992-00

62 EMLYN HUGHES, Defender, 1969-80

62 CHRIS WADDLE, Midfielder, 1985-91

62 DAVID PLATT, Midfielder, 1989-96

62 EMILE HESKEY, Striker, 1999-10

61 RAY CLEMENCE, Keeper, 1972-83

59 PETER BEARDSLEY, Forward, 1986-96

59 DES WALKER, Defender, 1988-93

59 PHIL NEVILLE, Defender, 1996-07

57 JIMMY GREAVES, Striker, 1959-67

57 PAUL GASCOIGNE, Midfielder, 1988-98

57 GARETH SOUTHGATE, Defender, 1995-04

56 JOHNNY HAYNES, Forward, 1964-62

56 JOE COLE, Midfielder, 2001-

54 STANLEY MATTHEWS, Forward, 1934-57

54 JERMAIN DEFOE, Striker, 2004-

53 GLENN HODDLE, Midfielder, 1979-88

53 PAUL INCE, Midfielder, 1992-00

53 DAVID JAMES, Keeper, 1997-10

53 GARETH BARRY, Midfielder, 2000-

52 TREVOR FRANCIS, Striker, 1977-86

51 TEDDY SHERINGHAM, Striker, 1993-02

50 PHIL NEAL, Defender, 1976-83

*Correct up to July 1, 2013

FOOTBALL LEGENDS

It's a word often over-used to describe good footballers. But the stars over the next pages can genuinely be regarded as legends. They have made their mark on the game and left fans many memories. There are other players who deserve high praise but these are Shoot's pick of the best...

PELE

Fact File

EDISON ARANTES DO NASCIMENTO

POSITION: Forward
HEIGHT: 1.73m (5ft 8 in)
BIRTH DATE: October 23, 1940
BIRTH PLACE: Tres Coracoes, Brazil
CLUBS: Santos, New York Cosmos
INTERNATIONAL: Brazil (92 **CAPS**, 77 goals)
PRO CAREER: 1956-77
WHY IS HE A LEGEND? Just look at his international stats! Plus, Pele scored 1,033 goals in 1,120 club appearances and is regarded by many fellow professionals as one of the best players ever.

MICHEL PLATINI

Fact File

MICHEL FRANCOIS PLATINI

POSITION: Midfielder
BIRTH DATE: June 21, 1955
BIRTH PLACE: Joeuf, France
HEIGHT: 1.78m (5ft 10in)
CLUBS: Nancy, Saint Etienne, Juventus
INTERNATIONAL: France (72 caps, 41 goals)
PRO CAREER: 1972-87
WHY IS HE A LEGEND: Now noted for his role as an official of UEFA, Platini was European Footballer of the Year in 1984, twice winner of both the Ballon d'Or and French Player of the Year. He also helped France win the the 1984 European Championships where he was their top scorer and Player of the Tournament.

FRANZ
BECKENBAUER
Fact File

FRANZ ANTON BECKENBAUER

POSITION: Defender
BIRTH DATE: September 11, 1945
BIRTH PLACE: Munich
HEIGHT: 1.81m (5ft 11in)
CLUBS: Bayern Munich New York Cosmos, Hamburg
INTERNATIONAL: Germany (103 caps, 14 goals)
PRO CAREER: 1964-83
WHY IS HE A LEGEND? The man known as Der Kaiser won the World Cup as a player (1974) and manager (1990). He also won the German Bundesliga as a Bayern Munich player (1969, 1972, 1973, 1974) and Hamburg (1982). He also won the Bundesliga as Bayern manager in 1994; and France's Ligue 1 as boss of Marseille (1991).

JOHAN CRUYFF

Fact File

HENDRIK JOHANNES CRUYFF

POSITION: Forward
BIRTH DATE: April 25, 1947
BIRTH PLACE: Amsterdam
HEIGHT: 1.8m (5ft 11in)
CLUBS: Ajax, Barcelona, LA Aztecs, Washington Diplomats, Levante, Ajax, Feyenoord
INTERNATIONAL: Holland
PRO CAREER: 1964-84
WHY IS HE A LEGEND? As a player he won the Ballon d'Or three times (1971, 1973, 1974); the Dutch Eredivisie on eight occasions with Ajax (1966, 1967, 1968, 1970, 1972, 1973, 1982, 1983) and once with Feyenoord (1984); Spain's La Liga with Barcelona (1974). As a manager he twice lifted the Dutch Cup with Ajax (1986,1987) and the UEFA Cup Winners' Cup (1987); at Barcelona he won La Liga four times (1991, 1992, 1993, 1994) plus the Copa del Rey (1990), Spanish Supercup (1991, 1992, 1994), European Cup (1992), Cup Winners' Cup (1989) and UEFA Super Cup (1992).

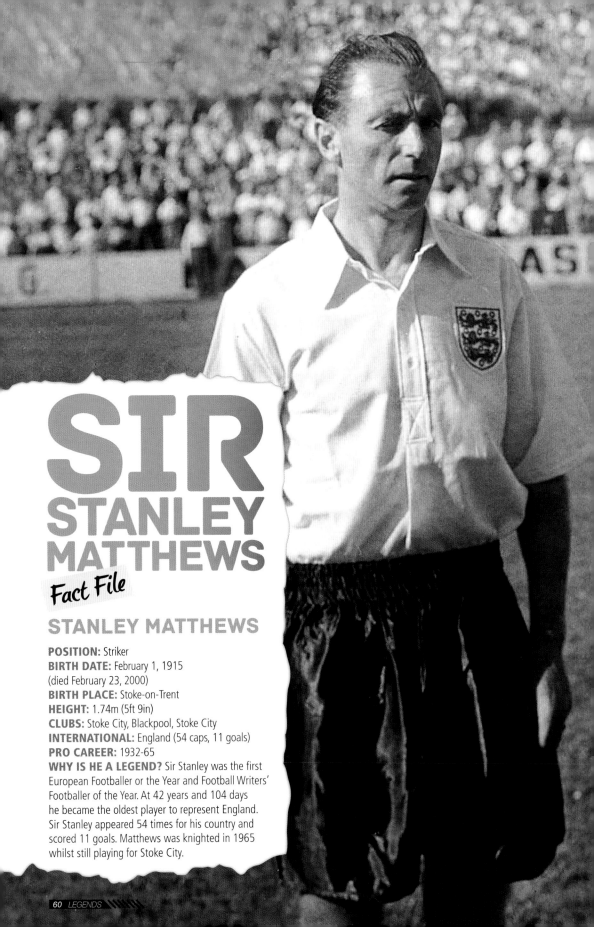

SIR
STANLEY
MATTHEWS
Fact File

STANLEY MATTHEWS

POSITION: Striker
BIRTH DATE: February 1, 1915
(died February 23, 2000)
BIRTH PLACE: Stoke-on-Trent
HEIGHT: 1.74m (5ft 9in)
CLUBS: Stoke City, Blackpool, Stoke City
INTERNATIONAL: England (54 caps, 11 goals)
PRO CAREER: 1932-65
WHY IS HE A LEGEND? Sir Stanley was the first
European Footballer or the Year and Football Writers'
Footballer of the Year. At 42 years and 104 days
he became the oldest player to represent England.
Sir Stanley appeared 54 times for his country and
scored 11 goals. Matthews was knighted in 1965
whilst still playing for Stoke City.

SIR GEOFF HURST

Fact File

GEOFFREY CHARLES HURST

POSITION: Striker
BIRTH DATE: December 8, 1941
BIRTH PLACE: Ashton-under-Lyne, Cheshire
HEIGHT: 1.81m (5ft 11in)
CLUBS: West Ham, Stoke City, Cape Town City (loan), West Brom, Cork Celtic, Seattle Sounders, Kuwait SC,
INTERNATIONAL: England (49 caps, 24 goals)
PRO CAREER: 1959-76
WHY IS HE A LEGEND? The only player to score a hat-trick in a World Cup Final – as England beat Germany 4-2 in 1966. Sir Geoff also won the European Cup Winners' Cup (1965) and FA Cup (1964) during his time with West Ham. Knighted in 1998.

DIEGO
MARADONA
Fact File

DIEGO ARMANDO MARADONA

POSITION: Forward
BIRTH DATE: October 31, 1960
BIRTH PLACE: Buenos Aires, Argentina
HEIGHT: 1.65m (5ft 5in)
CLUBS: Argentinos Juniors, Boca Juniors, Barcelona, Napoli, Sevilla, Newell's Old Boys, Boca Juniors
INTERNATIONAL: Argentina (91 games, 34 goals)
PRO CAREER: 1976-97
WHY IS HE A LEGEND? Ignore the infamous "Hand of God" goal when he pushed the ball into the net against England at the 1986 World Cup Finals, and Maradona is quite simply one of the best ball players ever. Former World Player of the Year, twice South American Player of the Year and twice a winner of Serie A with Napoli.

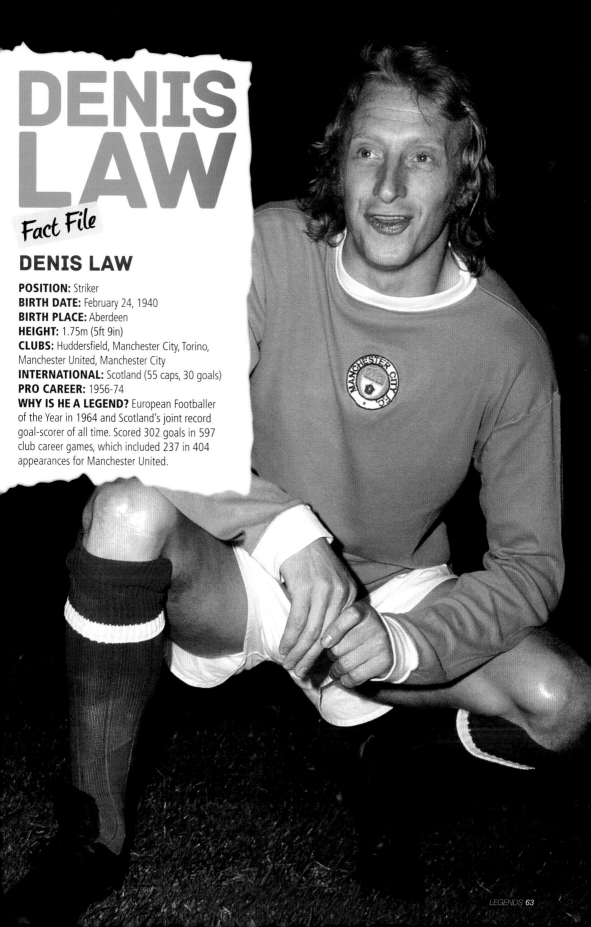

DENIS LAW

Fact File

DENIS LAW

POSITION: Striker
BIRTH DATE: February 24, 1940
BIRTH PLACE: Aberdeen
HEIGHT: 1.75m (5ft 9in)
CLUBS: Huddersfield, Manchester City, Torino, Manchester United, Manchester City
INTERNATIONAL: Scotland (55 caps, 30 goals)
PRO CAREER: 1956-74
WHY IS HE A LEGEND? European Footballer of the Year in 1964 and Scotland's joint record goal-scorer of all time. Scored 302 goals in 597 club career games, which included 237 in 404 appearances for Manchester United.

MARCO VAN BASTEN

Fact File

MARCEL VAN BASTEN

POSITION: Striker
BIRTH DATE: October 31, 1964
BIRTH PLACE: Utrecht, Holland
HEIGHT: 1.88m (6ft 2in)
CLUBS: Ajax, AC Milan
INTERNATIONAL: Holland (58 caps, 24 goals)
PRO CAREER: 1982-95
WHY IS HE A LEGEND? Van Basten's career was halted at the age of 28 when he had already built a massive reputation as a goal scorer with 278 in 376 club games. The 1985 Dutch Footballer of the Year was also the Eredivisie's top scorer in 1984, 1985, 1986 and 1987 and winner of the European and World Golden Boots (both 1986).

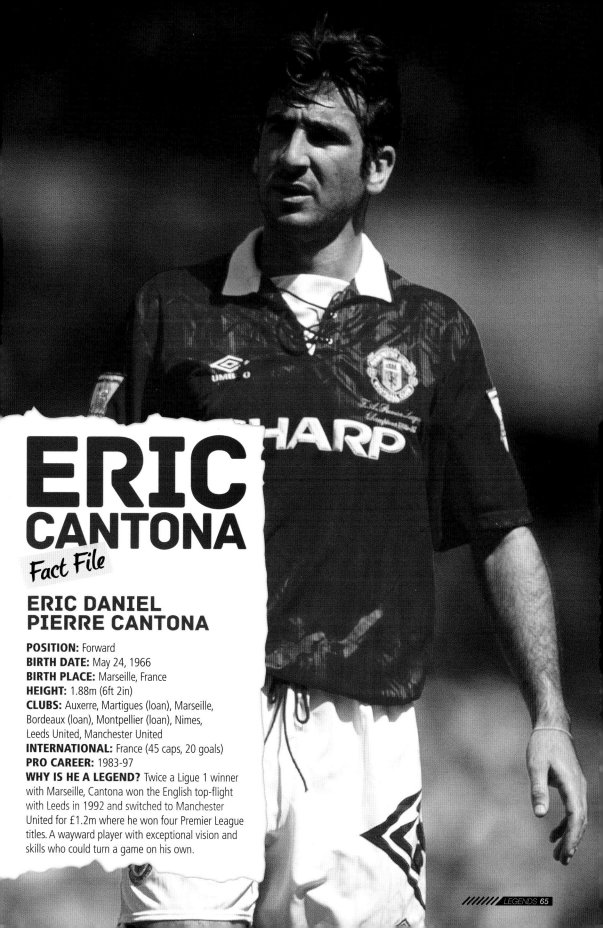

ERIC
CANTONA
Fact File

ERIC DANIEL PIERRE CANTONA

POSITION: Forward
BIRTH DATE: May 24, 1966
BIRTH PLACE: Marseille, France
HEIGHT: 1.88m (6ft 2in)
CLUBS: Auxerre, Martigues (loan), Marseille, Bordeaux (loan), Montpellier (loan), Nimes, Leeds United, Manchester United
INTERNATIONAL: France (45 caps, 20 goals)
PRO CAREER: 1983-97
WHY IS HE A LEGEND? Twice a Ligue 1 winner with Marseille, Cantona won the English top-flight with Leeds in 1992 and switched to Manchester United for £1.2m where he won four Premier League titles. A wayward player with exceptional vision and skills who could turn a game on his own.

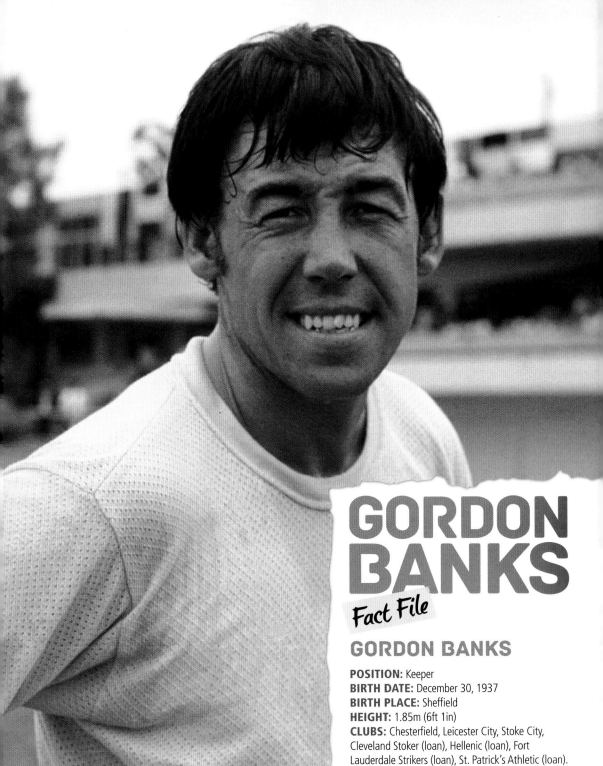

GORDON BANKS

GORDON BANKS

POSITION: Keeper
BIRTH DATE: December 30, 1937
BIRTH PLACE: Sheffield
HEIGHT: 1.85m (6ft 1in)
CLUBS: Chesterfield, Leicester City, Stoke City, Cleveland Stoker (loan), Hellenic (loan), Fort Lauderdale Strikers (loan), St. Patrick's Athletic (loan).
INTERNATIONAL: England (73 caps, 0 goals)
PRO CAREER: 1955-77
WHY IS HE A LEGEND? Banks made 628 club appearances, was FIFA Goalkeeper of the Year on six occasions and Football Writers' Footballer of the Year in 1972. Awarded an OBE in 1970.

BOBBY MOORE

Fact File

ROBERT FREDERICK CHELSEA MOORE

POSITION: Defender
BIRTH DATE: April 12, 1941 (died February 24, 1993)
BIRTH PLACE: Barking, Essex
HEIGHT: 1.87m (6ft 2in)
CLUBS: West Ham, Fulham, San Antonio Thunder, Seattle Sounders, Herning Fremad
INTERNATIONAL: England (108 caps, 2 goals)
PRO CAREER: 1958-78
WHY IS HE A LEGEND? Moore was captain of England when the team won the 1966 World Cup at Wembley and a statue of him stands outside the main entrance to the new stadium. He is rated as one of the calmest and most efficient defenders ever to play football. A UEFA Cup Winners' Cup and FA Cup-winner with West Ham. Awarded OBE in 1967.

GERD MULLER

Fact File

GERHARD MULLER

POSITION: Striker
BIRTH DATE: November 3, 1945
BIRTH PLACE: Nordlingen, Germany
HEIGHT: 1.76m (5ft 9in)
CLUBS: Nordlingen, Bayern Munich,
Ford Lauderdale Strikers
INTERNATIONAL: Germany (62 caps, 68 goals)
PRO CAREER: 1963-81
WHY IS HE A LEGEND? Muller's international
goals tally is a Germany record. He also hit 364 goals
in 427 Bundesliga games and 66 in 74 European
matches and was seven times the top scorer in his
country. German Footballer of the Year in 1967 and
1969, he won the European player award in 1970.

RONALDO
Fact File

RONALDO LUIS NAZARIO DE LIMA

POSITION: Striker
BIRTH DATE: September 22, 1976
BIRTH PLACE: Rio de Janeiro, Brazil
HEIGHT: 1.83m (6ft)
CLUBS: Cruzeiro, PSV Eindhoven, Barcelona, Inter Milan, Real Madrid, AC Milan, Corinthians
INTERNATIONAL: Brazil (98 caps, 62 goals)
PRO CAREER: 1993-11
WHY IS HE A LEGEND? Three times World Player of the Year (1996, 1997, 2002) he also won the Ballon d'Or twice (1997, 2002) and scored a record 15 goals at World Cup finals. Won the 2002 World Cup and silverware with all of his clubs.

PETER
SCHMEICHEL
Fact File

PETER BOLESLAW
SCHMEICHEL

POSITION: Keeper
BIRTH DATE: November 18, 1963
BIRTH PLACE: Gladsaxe, Denmark
HEIGHT: 1.91m (6ft 3in)
CLUBS: Brondby, Manchester United,
Sporting Lisbon, Aston Villa, Manchester City
INTERNATIONAL: Denmark (129 games, 1 goal)
PRO CAREER: 1987-03
WHY IS HE A LEGEND? Twice voted the World's
Best Goalkeeper (1992, 1993), four times UEFA
Goalkeeper of the Year (1992, 1993, 1997, 1998),
three times Denmark Football Player of the Year
(1990, 1993, 1999), he also won five Premier League
titles with Manchester United. Schmeichel was also
a member of the United side that won the Treble
of league, FA Cup and European Cup in 1999.

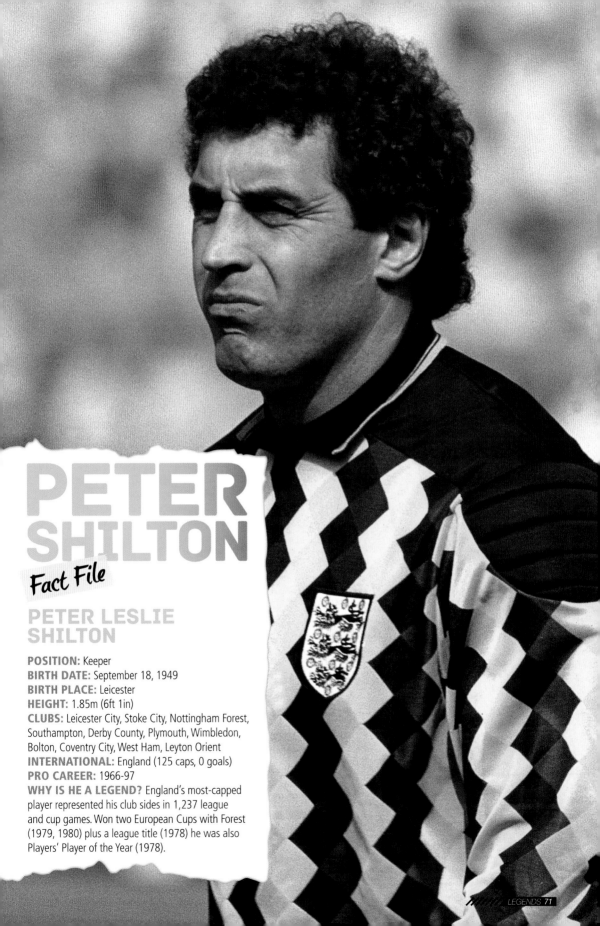

PETER SHILTON

Fact File

PETER LESLIE SHILTON

POSITION: Keeper
BIRTH DATE: September 18, 1949
BIRTH PLACE: Leicester
HEIGHT: 1.85m (6ft 1in)
CLUBS: Leicester City, Stoke City, Nottingham Forest, Southampton, Derby County, Plymouth, Wimbledon, Bolton, Coventry City, West Ham, Leyton Orient
INTERNATIONAL: England (125 caps, 0 goals)
PRO CAREER: 1966-97
WHY IS HE A LEGEND? England's most-capped player represented his club sides in 1,237 league and cup games. Won two European Cups with Forest (1979, 1980) plus a league title (1978) he was also Players' Player of the Year (1978).

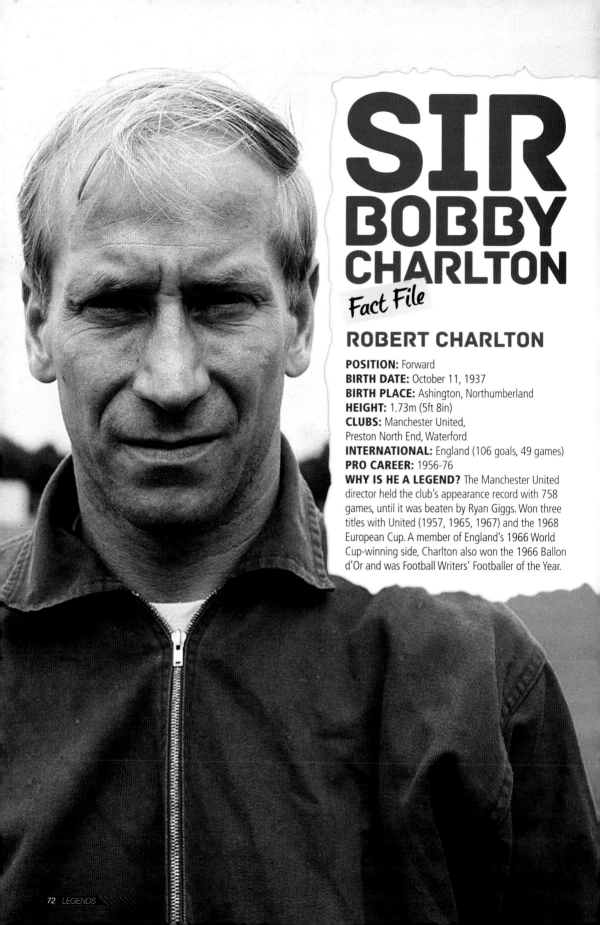

SIR BOBBY CHARLTON

Fact File

ROBERT CHARLTON

POSITION: Forward
BIRTH DATE: October 11, 1937
BIRTH PLACE: Ashington, Northumberland
HEIGHT: 1.73m (5ft 8in)
CLUBS: Manchester United, Preston North End, Waterford
INTERNATIONAL: England (106 goals, 49 games)
PRO CAREER: 1956-76
WHY IS HE A LEGEND? The Manchester United director held the club's appearance record with 758 games, until it was beaten by Ryan Giggs. Won three titles with United (1957, 1965, 1967) and the 1968 European Cup. A member of England's 1966 World Cup-winning side, Charlton also won the 1966 Ballon d'Or and was Football Writers' Footballer of the Year.

PAOLO MALDINI

Fact File

PAOLO CESARE MALDINI

POSITION: Defender
BIRTHDATE: June 26, 1968
BIRTHPLACE: Milan, Italy
HEIGHT: 1.86m (6ft 1in)
CLUBS: AC Milan
INTERNATIONAL: Italy (126 caps, 7 goals)
PRO CAREER: 1985-09
WHY IS HE A LEGEND? He spent his career with AC Milan notching 902 appearances until he retired just before his 41st birthday. Won seven Serie A titles (1988, 1992, 1993, 1994, 1996, 1999, 2004) five Champions Leagues (1989, 1990, 1994, 2003, 2007) and played a record 168 games for Milan in European competitions.

EUSEBIO
Fact File

EUSEBIO DA SILVA FERREIRA

POSITION: Forward
BIRTH DATE: January 25, 1942
BIRTH PLACE: Lourenco Marques, East Africa
HEIGHT: 1.75m (5ft 9in)
CLUBS: Sporting de Lourenco Marques, Benfica, Boston Minutemen, Monterrey, Toronto Metros, Beira-Mar, Las Vegas Quicksilvers, Uniao de Tomar, New Jersey Americans
INTERNATIONAL: Portugal (64 caps, 41 goals)
PRO CAREER: 1957-79
WHY IS HE A LEGEND? Eusebio won 11 Portuguese titles with Benfica (1961, 1963, 1964, 1965, 1967, 1968, 1969, 1971, 1972, 1973, 1975). He played 614 games for the club and scored a record 638 goals. Eusebio also won five Portuguese Cups (1962, 1964, 1969, 1970, 1972) and a European Cup (1962). The 1965 European Footballer of the Year also won the Golden Boot twice (1968, 1973).

PUSKAS
Fact File

FERENC PUSKAS

POSITION: Midfielder
BIRTH DATE: April 1, 1927
(died November 17, 2006)
BIRTH PLACE: Budapest, Hungary
HEIGHT: 1.69m (5ft 7in)
CLUBS: Budapest Honved, Real Madrid
INTERNATIONAL: Hungary (85 caps, 84 goals);
Spain (4 caps, 0 goals)
PRO CAREER: 1943-1966
WHY IS HE A LEGEND? Five times a league
winner in Hungary (1949, 1950, 1952, 1954, 1955)
Puskas also won the title on five occasions in Spain
(1961, 1962, 1963, 1964, 1965). European Player of
the Year (1953), Hungary's Player of the 20th Century,
four times top scorer in his homeland and an Olympic
gold medallist (1952).

GEORGE BEST

Fact File

GEORGE BEST

POSITION: Midfielder
BIRTH DATE: May 22, 1946 (died November 25, 2005)
BIRTH PLACE: Belfast, Northern Ireland
HEIGHT: 1.75m (5ft 9in)
CLUBS: Manchester United, Los Angeles Aztecs, Fulham, Fort Lauderdale Strikers, Hibernian, San Jose Earthquakes, Bournemouth
INTERNATIONAL: Northern Ireland (37 games, 9 goals).
PRO CAREER: 1963-83
WHY IS HE A LEGEND? Arguably football's first celebrity player, Best's skills were amazing. Won the European Cup with Manchester United in1968, the same year he was named both European and Football Writers' Footballer of the Year. Scored 179 goals in 470 games for the Red Devils where he won two league titles (1965, 1967).

ENGLAND'S
TOP-FLIGHT STARS

Check out the greatest players from England's top division. These are the
Professional Footballers' Association's most admired stars with an in-depth
look at all seasons of the Premier League since it began in 1992-93

PFA TEAMS

Pat Jennings,
Tottenham Hotspur

1976

GK Pat Jennings, Tottenham Hotspur
DF Paul Madeley, Leeds United
DF Roy McFarland, Derby County
DF Kevin Beattie, Ipswich Town
DF Colin Todd, Derby County
MF Kevin Keegan, Liverpool
MF Don Masson, QPR
MF Alan Hudson, Stoke City
FW Duncan McKenzie, Leeds United
FW John Toshack, Liverpool
FW Dennis Tueart, Manchester City

Kevin Beattie,
Ipswich Town

1974

GK Pat Jennings, Tottenham Hotspur
DF Paul Madeley, Leeds United
DF Roy McFarland, Derby County
DF Norman Hunter, Leeds United
DF Colin Todd, Derby County
MF Billy Bremner, Leeds United
MF Tony Currie, Sheffield United
MF Johnny Giles, Leeds United
FW Mick Channon, Southampton
FW Malcolm Macdonald, Newcastle United
FW Allan Clarke, Leeds United

1977

Kevin Keegan,
Liverpool

1978

GK Peter Shilton, Nottingham Forest
DF John Gidman, Aston Villa
DF Gordon McQueen, Leeds United
DF Martin Buchan, Manchester United
DF Derek Statham, West Bromwich Albion
MF Steve Coppell, Manchester United
MF Liam Brady, Arsenal
MF Trevor Brooking, West Ham United
FW Trevor Francis, Birmingham City
FW Joe Jordan, Manchester United
FW John Robertson, Nottingham Forest

1975

GK Peter Shilton, Stoke City
DF Paul Madeley, Leeds United
DF Gordon McQueen, Leeds United
DF Kevin Beattie, Ipswich Town
DF Colin Todd, Derby County
MF Billy Bonds, West Ham United
MF Colin Bell, Manchester City
MF Alan Hudson, Stoke City
FW Duncan McKenzie, Leeds United
FW Bob Latchford, Everton
FW Leighton James, Burnley

GK Ray Clemence, Liverpool
DF John Gidman, Aston Villa
DF Roy McFarland, Derby County
DF Kevin Beattie, Ipswich Town
DF Mick Mills, Ipswich Town
MF Kevin Keegan, Liverpool
MF Brian Talbot, Ipswich Town
MF Trevor Brooking, West Ham United
FW Trevor Francis, Birmingham City
FW Andy Gray, Aston Villa
FW Dennis Tueart, Manchester City

Steve Coppell,
Manchester United

1979

GK Peter Shilton, Nottingham Forest
DF Viv Anderson, Nottingham Forest
DF David O'Leary, Arsenal
DF Dave Watson, Manchester City
DF Derek Statham,
West Bromwich Albion
MF Tony Currie, Leeds United
MF Liam Brady, Arsenal

Dave Watson,
Manchester City

Gary Shaw,
Aston Villa

Liam Brady,
Arsenal

MF Osvaldo Ardiles,
Tottenham Hotspur
FW Cyrille Regis,
West Bromwich Albion
FW Kenny Dalglish, Liverpool
FW Laurie Cunningham,
West Bromwich Albion

1980

GK Peter Shilton, Nottingham Forest
DF Viv Anderson, Nottingham Forest
DF David O'Leary, Arsenal
DF Dave Watson, Southampton
DF Kenny Sansom, Crystal Palace
MF Terry McDermott, Liverpool
MF Liam Brady, Arsenal

MF Glenn Hoddle,
Tottenham Hotspur
FW David Johnson, Liverpool
FW Kenny Dalglish, Liverpool
FW Garry Birtles, Nottingham Forest

1981

GK Peter Shilton, Nottingham Forest
DF Kenny Swain, Aston Villa
DF Russell Osman, Ipswich Town
DF Allan Evans, Aston Villa
DF Kenny Sansom, Arsenal
MF Frans Thijssen, Ipswich Town
MF John Wark, Ipswich Town

Peter Shilton,
Nottingham Forest

MF Graeme Souness, Liverpool
FW Paul Mariner, Ipswich Town
FW Kenny Dalglish, Liverpool
FW Gary Shaw, Aston Villa

1982

GK Peter Shilton, Nottingham Forest
DF Kenny Swain, Aston Villa
DF David O'Leary, Arsenal
DF Alan Hansen, Liverpool
DF Kenny Sansom, Arsenal
MF Glenn Hoddle,
Tottenham Hotspur
MF Bryan Robson,
Manchester United
MF Graeme Souness, Liverpool

Bryan Robson,
Manchester United

Trevor Francis,
Manchester City

FW Trevor Francis, Manchester City
FW Kevin Keegan, Liverpool
FW Cyrille Regis,
    West Bromwich Albion

1983

GK Peter Shilton, Southampton
DF Dennis Thomas, Coventry City
DF Mark Lawrenson, Liverpool
DF Alan Hansen, Liverpool
DF Kenny Sansom, Arsenal

Mark Lawrenson,
Liverpool

MF Sammy Lee, Liverpool
MF Bryan Robson,
    Manchester United
MF Graeme Souness, Liverpool
FW Ian Rush, Liverpool
FW Kenny Dalglish, Liverpool
FW Steve Coppell,
    Manchester United

1984

GK Peter Shilton, Southampton
DF Mike Duxberry,
    Manchester United
DF Mark Lawrenson, Liverpool
DF Alan Hansen, Liverpool
DF Kenny Sansom, Arsenal
MF Glenn Hoddle,
    Tottenham Hotspur
MF Bryan Robson,
    Manchester United
MF Graeme Souness, Liverpool
FW Ian Rush, Liverpool
FW Kenny Dalglish, Liverpool
FW Frank Stapleton,
    Manchester United

1985

GK Peter Shilton, Southampton
DF Gary Stevens, Everton
DF Mark Lawrenson, Liverpool
DF Kevin Ratcliffe, Everton
DF Kenny Sansom, Arsenal
MF Peter Reid, Everton
MF Bryan Robson,
    Manchester United
MF Kevin Sheedy, Everton
FW Ian Rush, Liverpool
FW Chris Waddle, Newcastle United
FW Kerry Dixon, Chelsea

Chris Waddle,
Newcastle United

Kerry Dixon,
Chelsea

1986

GK Peter Shilton, Southampton
DF Gary Stevens, Everton
DF Mark Lawrenson, Liverpool
DF Paul McGrath,
    Manchester United
DF Kenny Sansom, Arsenal
MF Glenn Hoddle,
    Tottenham Hotspur
MF Bryan Robson,
    Manchester United
MF Stewart Robson, Arsenal
FW Gary Lineker, Everton
FW Mark Hughes,
    Manchester United
FW Paul Walsh, Liverpool

1987

GK Neville Southall, Everton
DF Viv Anderson, Arsenal
DF Alan Hansen, Liverpool
DF Tony Adams, Arsenal
DF Kenny Sansom, Arsenal
MF Glenn Hoddle,
    Tottenham Hotspur
MF David Rocastle, Arsenal
MF Kevin Sheedy, Everton
FW Ian Rush, Liverpool
FW Clive Allen, Tottenham Hotspur
FW Peter Beardsley,
    Newcastle United

1988

GK Neville Southall, Everton
DF Gary Stevens, Everton
DF Alan Hansen, Liverpool
DF Gary Gillespie, Liverpool
DF Stuart Pearce, Nottingham Forest
MF Steve McMahon, Liverpool
MF Peter Reid, Everton
MF Paul Gascoigne,
Newcastle United
MF John Barnes, Liverpool
FW Graeme Sharp, Everton
FW Peter Beardsley, Liverpool

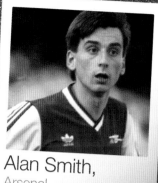

Alan Smith,
Arsenal

1990

GK Neville Southall, Everton
DF Lee Dixon, Arsenal
DF Des Walker, Nottingham Forest
DF Alan Hansen, Liverpool
DF Stuart Pearce, Nottingham Forest
MF David Platt, Aston Villa
MF Steve Hodge, Nottingham Forest
MF Steve McMahon, Liverpool
MF John Barnes, Liverpool
FW Peter Beardsley, Liverpool
FW Gary Lineker, Tottenham Hotspur

Graeme Sharp,
Everton

1989

GK Neville Southall, Everton
DF Steve Nicol, Liverpool
DF Des Walker, Nottingham Forest
DF Paul Parker, QPR
DF Stuart Pearce, Nottingham Forest
MF David Rocastle, Arsenal
MF Bryan Robson,
Manchester United
MF Andy Townsend, Norwich City
MF Chris Waddle,
Tottenham Hotspur
FW Mark Hughes,
Manchester United
FW Alan Smith, Arsenal

1991

GK David Seaman, Arsenal
DF Lee Dixon, Arsenal
DF Des Walker, Nottingham Forest

Des Walker,
Nottingham Forest

DF Mark Wright, Derby County
DF Stuart Pearce, Nottingham Forest
MF Gordon Strachan, Leeds United
MF Paul Gascoigne,
Tottenham Hotspur
MF Andy Townsend, Chelsea
MF John Barnes, Liverpool
FW Mark Hughes,
Manchester United
FW Ian Rush, Liverpool

Ian Rush,
Liverpool

1992

GK Tony Coton, Manchester City
DF Rob Jones, Liverpool
DF Gary Pallister, Manchester United
DF Des Walker, Nottingham Forest
DF Stuart Pearce, Nottingham Forest
MF Ray Houghton, Liverpool
MF Gary McAllister, Leeds United
MF Andy Townsend, Chelsea
FW Gary Lineker, Tottenham Hotspur
FW Mark Hughes,
Manchester United
FW Alan Shearer, Southampton

Turn over to
see who makes
the list from
1993 to 2013

PFA TEAM OF THE YEAR 1992-1993

Peter Schmeichel,
Manchester United

Included in the team of the year after his shot-stopping exploits helped United lift the inaugural Premier League title, and first top-flight crown since 1967. Played all 42 games, conceding just 31 times, as the Red Devils won the division by ten points.

PFA APPEARANCES: 1

David Bardsley,
QPR

The defender's impressive showings for the Rs earned him two England caps under Graham Taylor. Played 40 matches as his side finished fifth in the table. As well as being solid defensively, he contributed three goals this campaign.

PFA APPEARANCES: 1

Paul McGrath,
Aston Villa

The Irishman had an outstanding year and was named PFA Player of the Season. Played all 42 matches as Villa finished second. Was part of the side's backline that conceded just 40 goals — the second best in the division. Scored four times, including home and away against Middlesbrough.

PFA APPEARANCES: 2

Gary Pallister,
Manchester United

Pallister formed an impressive partnership with Steve Bruce at the back as United conceded just 31 goals on their way to the championship. The former England man played all 42 games and scored against Blackburn Rovers in the final home game of the season.

PFA APPEARANCES: 2

Tony Dorigo,
Leeds United

Despite Leeds finishing 17th, there was no doubt that Dorigo's performances helped his side survive the drop. The England international played 33 league matches and produced numerous impressive defensive displays. Scored the vital winner and his only goal of the season against Ipswich in February.

PFA APPEARANCES: 1

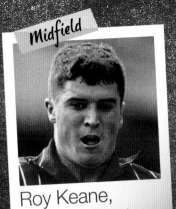

Midfield

Roy Keane,
Nottingham Forest

The 21-year-old showed his class in many of the 40 league games he played in the Forest midfield. The Reds were relegated, but the performances of Keano led to a British record £3.75m move to Manchester United. The Irishman scored six goals, including two at Leeds and one at Arsenal.

PFA APPEARANCES: 1

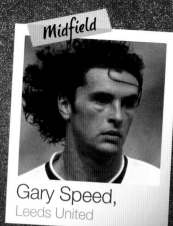

Midfield

Gary Speed,
Leeds United

The Wales international was another player who impressed during a disappointing season for Leeds. The 22-year-old's all-action displays saw him notch seven goals in 39 appearances. Scored vital goals, home and away, against Southampton.

PFA APPEARANCES: 1

Midfield

Paul Ince,
Manchester United

United's midfield general played all but one of the season's league games as United claimed the title. His tough tackling and class on the ball were key components in capturing the championship. Scored in the final three games of the season and in the derby against Manchester City at Old Trafford. Ince's form earned him an England debut in September 1992.

PFA APPEARANCES: 1

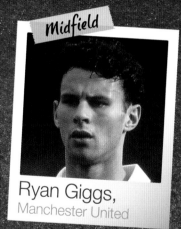

Midfield

Ryan Giggs,
Manchester United

The 19-year-old winger earned a first appearance in the PFA XI after playing in all but one of United's league games. The Wales international's nine goals, pace and creativity saw him retain the PFA Young Player of the Year Award. Hit two vital strikes against Southampton in February as United took another step towards the title.

PFA APPEARANCES: 1

Forward

Ian Wright,
Arsenal

The England striker helped Arsenal to a tenth placed finish and the FA Cup by firing 17 goals. Scored in both the final and the replay against Sheffield Wednesday, and hit important league goals against Liverpool, Wimbledon, Manchester City and Chelsea. His movement and ruthlessness in front of goal proved a constant thorn for opposition defences.

PFA APPEARANCES: 1

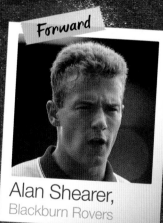

Forward

Alan Shearer,
Blackburn Rovers

The 22-year-old hit 16 league goals in just 21 matches during his debut season with Rovers. Scored vital goals against Liverpool, Leeds and Arsenal, as his side finished fourth, just one point outside the European qualification spots. Shearer was also selected for the PFA XI the previous season after making his England debut in February 1992.

PFA APPEARANCES: 2

PFA TEAM OF THE YEAR 1993-1994

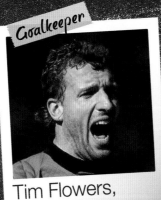

Goalkeeper

Tim Flowers,
Blackburn Rovers

The smart stopper earned a first selection into the best XI with a number of impressive displays. Conceded just 23 goals in his 30 league games as Rovers finished runners-up. The 25-year-old's form in his debut season at Ewood Park saw him handed an England debut.

PFA APPEARANCES: 1

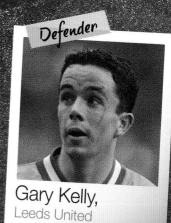

Defender

Gary Kelly,
Leeds United

Kelly impressed in his breakthrough season at Elland Road, playing all 42 league games as Leeds secured fifth place. The Irishman was a huge part of the backline that had the fourth best defensive record in the division with just 39 goals against.

PFA APPEARANCES: 1

Defender

Gary Pallister,
Manchester United

Pallister was included in the PFA side for a third time after helping United claim a league and FA Cup double. The England man, who contributed one goal, marshaled a defence that conceded 38 goals on their way to defending the title.

PFA APPEARANCES: 3

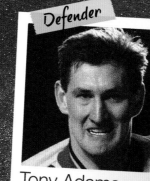

Defender

Tony Adams,
Arsenal

The England and Arsenal captain played 35 league games in a Gunners defence that conceded just 28 goals – the best in the division. The 26-year-old was dominant in the air and on the ground as Arsenal finished fourth.

PFA APPEARANCES: 2

Defender

Denis Irwin,
Manchester United

Irwin carried on his impressive form from the previous year, which saw him play 40 times for United. This time round he was an ever-present and scored twice, including one against Liverpool at Anfield. The Irishman's willingness to get forward and clever positioning was impresseive.

PFA APPEARANCES: 1

David Batty,
Blackburn Rovers

The tough tackling midfielder continued to make an impression at Leeds in the 1993-94 campaign. The 23-year-old was a tough opponent for anyone in his 36 league appearances. Formed a great partnership with Gary Speed and McAllister as United finished fifth.

PFA APPEARANCES: 1

Gary McAllister,
Leeds United

The Scot was simply unplayable at times in the Leeds midfield. A class act on the ball and tricky to beat off it, the 27-year-old was feared by many opponents. Chipped in with eight goals, including vital strikes against Liverpool, Arsenal and Blackburn Rovers.

PFA APPEARANCES: 2

Paul Ince,
Manchester United

The England man secured a place in the PFA XI midfield for the second successive year after collecting consecutive championship medals. The Guv'nor scored eight goals in 39 league appearances, including winners against Liverpool and Oldham Athletic.

PFA APPEARANCES: 2

Peter Beardsley,
Newcastle United

The playmaker impressed on his return to Newcastle, scoring 21 goals in 35 league matches. The 32-year-old grabbed a hat-trick against Wimbledon and five braces. United, who finished third, were the highest scorers in the division with 82 goals. Beardsley was sixth-top scorer in the league and created many of the 34 scored by team-mate Andy Cole.

PFA APPEARANCES: 4

Eric Cantona,
Manchester United

The Frenchman was simply a genius in his second season at Old Trafford. His 18 goals in 34 matches didn't tell half the story as his technique and flair baffled opponents. Scored two braces in the derbies against Manchester City, collected the PFA Player of the Year Award, and was the main reason United won the title by eight points.

PFA APPEARANCES: 1

Alan Shearer,
Blackburn Rovers

Shearer made it three inclusions on the bounce in the PFA team after firing 31 goals in 40 league matches. The England man was the league's second top scorer behind Newcastle's Andy Cole and scored nearly half of Blackburn's 63 goals that season.

PFA APPEARANCES: 3

PFA TEAM OF THE YEAR 1994-1995

Goalkeeper

Tim Flowers,
Blackburn Rovers

The Rovers shot-stopper made it two consecutive inclusions after helping his side lift their first top-flight title since 1914. The England man kept 16 clean sheets and conceded just 34 goals in 39 league appearances.

PFA APPEARANCES: 2

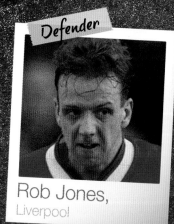

Defender

Rob Jones,
Liverpool

The defender was selected for a second time after helping Liverpool to fourth place with numerous solid defensive displays. The England international played 31 times in a defence that conceded just 37 times – the second best record in the division.

PFA APPEARANCES: 1

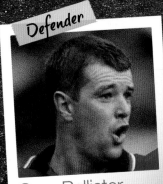

Defender

Gary Pallister,
Manchester United

The England man was selected for the fourth consecutive year after helping United to runner-up spot. The Red Devils finished a point behind Blackburn and conceded just 28 goals – the best in the league. Pallister played 35 league matches, scoring winners against Tottenham and Wimbledon.

PFA APPEARANCES: 4

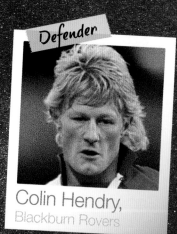

Defender

Colin Hendry,
Blackburn Rovers

The 29-year-old was different class during Rovers' title-winning season. Played 37 times in the league and scored four goals, including a vital winner against Aston Villa. Blackburn kept 13 clean sheets when the Scot was in the side.

PFA APPEARANCES: 1

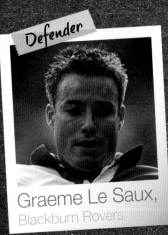

Defender

Graeme Le Saux,
Blackburn Rovers

The title-winning left back played 39 league games. Defensively solid and creative when going forward, the 26-year-old's form saw him become an established England international. Chipped in with three goals, including an important strike against Arsenal.

PFA APPEARANCES: 1

Midfield

Tim Sherwood,
Blackburn Rovers

Rovers' captain was magnificent as he guided his side to the title. Scored six times in 38 matches, including winners against Crystal Palace and Chelsea. His dogged, determined displays gave him the nickname 'The Grafter'.

PFA APPEARANCES: 1

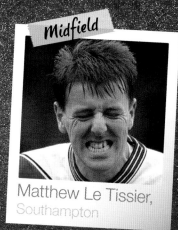

Midfield

Matthew Le Tissier,
Southampton

'Le God', as he was known by fans, once again excelled for the Hampshire side. The 26-year-old scored 19 league goals in 41 appearances, including two winning doubles against Tottenham. Was at the heartbeat of everything Saints did well, as they finished comfortably in 10th.

PFA APPEARANCES: 1

Midfield

Paul Ince,
Manchester United

The England warrior made it three PFA appearances in a row as he proved to be the heart of United once more. Scored five times in 36 matches, but was again the midfield shield that contributed to the Reds securing the best defensive record. Struck in United's 9-0 win over Ipswich – a Premier League record victory.

PFA APPEARANCES: 3

Forward

Jurgen Klinsmann,
Tottenham Hotspur

Klinsmann was a revelation during his first season in England. He scored 21 times in 41 games, including one against rivals Arsenal. The Germany international's technique and finishing ability made him an instant hit at White Hart Lane. Played a massive part in the club achieving a top-seven finish.

PFA APPEARANCES: 1

Forward

Chris Sutton,
Blackburn Rovers

Half of the SAS partnership with Alan Shearer, Sutton had an amazing debut season following his move from Norwich. Scored 15 times, but his unselfish movement and vision helped Shearer grab many goals. Hit a hat-trick against Coventry and a winner against QPR in April.

PFA APPEARANCES: 1

Forward

Alan Shearer,
Blackburn Rovers

Shearer made it four PFA selections in a row as he fired Rovers to the title. He was the division's top scorer with an incredible 34 goals, including three hat-tricks. Scored all types of goals and was voted PFA Player of the Year for the first time.

PFA APPEARANCES: 4

PFA TEAM OF THE YEAR 1995-1996

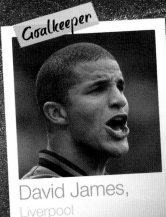

David James,
Liverpool

The Reds stopper conceded just 34 goals and kept 16 clean sheets throughout the league campaign as Liverpool finished third. The 25-year-old made a number of world-class saves during the campaign to earn a first selection into the PFA XI.

PFA APPEARANCES: 1

Defender

Gary Neville,
Manchester United

The United right back played a major part in his side regaining the title from Blackburn. Neville played 30 league matches in a defence that conceded just 35 times all season. His solid defensive displays also earned him a regular place in the England squad for Euro '96.

PFA APPEARANCES: 1

Defender

Tony Adams,
Arsenal

The Arsenal skipper guided the club to fifth. The Gunners conceded just 32 goals — the least in the division — mainly due to their captain's ability to marshal the backline. Adams was included despite only making 21 appearances and was appointed England captain prior to Euro '96.

PFA APPEARANCES: 3

Defender

Ugo Ehiogu,
Aston Villa

The 23-year-old was a rock at the heart of Villa's defence. Played 36 times in a side that conceded just 35 times — the same as champions Manchester United — and finished fourth. Scored the winner at Spurs, and saw his form rewarded with an England debut in May 1996.

PFA APPEARANCES: 1

Defender

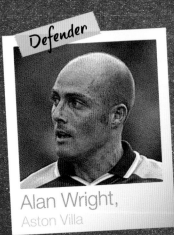

Alan Wright,
Aston Villa

Another solid Villa performer who forced his way into the PFA side after an impressive debut season at Villa Park. Played 38 times and scored in victories against Middlesbrough and Leeds. Wright was a threat going forwards but could always be relied upon to stop opposing wide men.

PFA APPEARANCES: 1

Midfield

Steve Stone,
Nottingham Forest

Forest's midfield maestro had a superb campaign and scored seven times in 34 appearances. His tireless work played a huge part in Forest securing a ninth placed finish. The 24-year-old's performances saw him selected for England's Euro '96 squad.

PFA APPEARANCES: 1

Midfield

Rob Lee,
Newcastle United

The technically gifted midfielder was a star performer in what was so nearly a title-winning season for Newcastle. Lee scored eight goals in 36 appearances, including a brace against Nottingham Forest. Lee was at the heart of most of the Magpies good attacking work.

PFA APPEARANCES: 1

Midfield

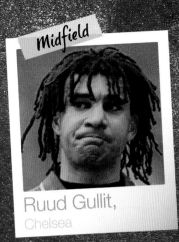

Ruud Gullit,
Chelsea

The 1987 Ballon d'Or winner lit up the Premier League in his debut season in England. The 33-year-old showed the class of his younger days, scoring three times in 33 appearances for the Blues. The Dutchman was the linchpin of the Chelsea midfield, and a bright spark in what was a disappointing season for the London club, as they finished 11th.

PFA APPEARANCES: 1

Midfield

David Ginola,
Newcastle United

The France winger was another player to star in his debut year in England. Ginola dazzled defences with his skill and technique. Struck five times in 34 appearances for runners-up Newcastle. Scored and played a major role in the famous 4-3 defeat at Liverpool, and excited fans with his attacking mindset and wonderful ability.

PFA APPEARANCES: 1

Forward

Les Ferdinand,
Newcastle United

The PFA Player of the Year was in stunning form for the Toon Army, and scored 25 goals in 37 matches to be the division's third highest scorer. The striker's tally fired Newcastle to second place and earned him a call-up to England's Euro '96 squad. His goals included a hat-trick against Wimbledon.

PFA APPEARANCES: 1

Forward

Alan Shearer,
Blackburn Rovers

The England star was selected for a fifth successive year after again claiming the division's Golden Boot award. Shearer struck 31 times for Rovers, but they were unable to defend the title, finishing seventh. Scored five hat-tricks and was included in England's Euro '96 squad.

PFA APPEARANCES: 5

PFA TEAM OF THE YEAR 1996-1997

Goalkeeper

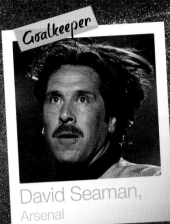

David Seaman,
Arsenal

Despite appearing just 22 times in the league, England's No.1 was voted as the best keeper after keeping ten clean sheets. Played a major part in Arsenal's defensive record – just 32 goals conceded all season – and made a number of world-class saves.

PFA APPEARANCES: 2

Defender

Gary Neville,
Manchester United

The England right back earned back-to-back inclusions after again impressing for United. Played 31 times and notched his first goal in the 3-3 draw against Middlesbrough, as the Red Devils claimed another Premier League title.

PFA APPEARANCES: 2

Defender

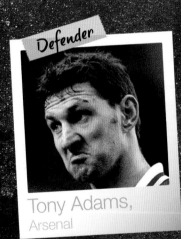

Tony Adams,
Arsenal

The Arsenal captain and England defender was a class apart in the 21 Premier League games he took part in. Scored in the 4-2 win over Southampton and was a dominant performer in defence, leading to a fourth inclusion. Arsenal finished third in their first season under Arsene Wenger.

PFA APPEARANCES: 4

Defender

Mark Wright,
Liverpool

The England international was selected for the second time – but for a different club – after a number of assured performances for the Reds. Played 33 times for the Merseysiders who had the second best defensive record in the league and finished fourth.

PFA APPEARANCES: 2

Defender

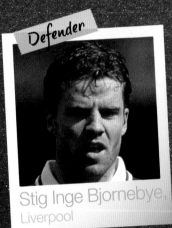

Stig Inge Bjornebye,
Liverpool

The Norway international was a highly consistent performer in the Liverpool backline. Played all 38 league matches and scored twice. The 27-year-old contributed in both attack and defence throughout the season.

PFA APPEARANCES: 1

Midfield
David Beckham,
Manchester United

Collected the PFA Young Player of the Year Award after a campaign in which he scored eight times in 36 league appearances. His goals included the winner against Liverpool and a strike from inside his own half against Wimbledon. Created many of United's 76 goals from set pieces. Handed an England debut in September 1996.

PFA APPEARANCES: 1

Midfield
Roy Keane,
Manchester United

The Republic of Ireland star again shone in the heart of the United midfield. Only played 21 league games, but his influence and leadership guided Alex Ferguson's side to the title. Scored two goals but was a dominant shield in front of the back four.

PFA APPEARANCES: 2

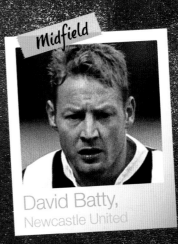

Midfield
David Batty,
Newcastle United

The tough tackler's second inclusion came after a bright debut season at Newcastle United. The England star's combative style in the 32 appearances he made helped the Magpies secure a second consecutive runner-up spot.

PFA APPEARANCES: 2

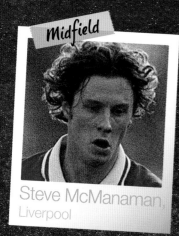

Midfield
Steve McManaman,
Liverpool

The Reds winger dazzled the Anfield crowd with his quick feet and eye for a goal. If he wasn't setting up his team-mates, he was finishing himself. The England man scored seven goals in 37 league games, which included a winning brace against Arsenal.

PFA APPEARANCES: 1

Forward
Ian Wright,
Arsenal

The division's second-highest scorer behind Alan Shearer, Arsenal's No. 9 hit the back of the net an incredible 23 times in 35 Premier League games. Hit a hat-trick in a 4-1 win against Blackburn, and struck up a great partnership with Dennis Bergkamp.

PFA APPEARANCES: 2

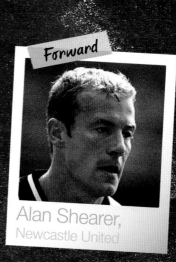

Forward
Alan Shearer,
Newcastle United

The £15m world record transfer man was selected for a sixth consecutive season after topping the goalscoring charts for a third year running. The England striker scored 25 league goals, including a hat-trick in a 4-3 win over Leicester, during his debut campaign for his hometown club.

PFA APPEARANCES: 6

PFA TEAM OF THE YEAR 1997-1998

Goalkeeper

Nigel Martyn,
Leeds United

The 31-year-old was selected for the first time after a fantastic second season at Elland Road. Kept 11 clean sheets in 37 matches as Leeds finished fifth. His form saw him included in England's 1998 World Cup squad where he was second choice behind David Seaman.

PFA APPEARANCES: 1

Defender

Gary Neville,
Manchester United

United's right back made it three inclusions in a row after yet another top season. Despite a trophyless campaign, Neville helped his side claim second place in the league with the best defensive record, conceding just 26 times. Part of England's 1998 World Cup side.

PFA APPEARANCES: 3

Defender

Gary Pallister,
Manchester United

Pallister impressed his fellow pros once more, despite failing to pick up any silverware. Was a rock at the heart of United's defence in all of his 33 appearances. Helped his side claim five consecutive clean sheets at the start of the season.

PFA APPEARANCES: 5

Defender

Colin Hendry,
Blackburn Rovers

The Rovers captain helped his side finish sixth after another impressive campaign. Made numerous blocks and vital interceptions in his 34 appearances. Selected as Scotland skipper for the 1998 World Cup. Moved to Rangers for £4m at the end of the campaign.

PFA APPEARANCES: 2

Defender

Graeme Le Saux,
Chelsea

The England left back was a consistent performer as the Blues enjoyed their best Premier League season to date, finishing fourth. Made 37 appearances in a campaign where the London side lifted the League Cup and European Cup Winners' Cup.

PFA APPEARANCES: 2

David Beckham,
Manchester United

The young England star was included again after another top-class season. Played a major part in helping United hit 73 goals – the most in the division, by supplying numerous quality crosses. Notched nine times himself. The 23-year-old's form saw him selected for the 1998 World Cup.

PFA APPEARANCES: 2

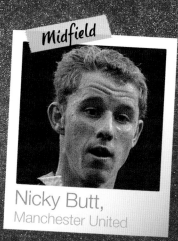

Nicky Butt,
Manchester United

The defensive midfielder was an unsung hero in an attacking United side. His good work was recognised by team-mates and opposition players who felt his 33 league appearances warranted a place in the PFA XI. Only scored three times but his desire to win and retain the ball helped United claim second spot.

PFA APPEARANCES: 1

David Batty,
Newcastle United

The Magpies battler was again recognised by his fellow pros after another productive season on Tyneside. Played 32 league games and scored the winner at Aston Villa. United finished a disappointing 13th but reached the FA Cup Final where they lost to Arsenal. Batty was selected for England's 1998 World Cup squad.

PFA APPEARANCES: 3

Ryan Giggs,
Manchester United

The Wales star scored eight goals in 29 games as United finished a point behind Arsenal. Hit doubles against Barnsley and Spurs, and used his pace to consistently fly pass full backs. Supplied eight of the Red Devils' 73 goals – the most in the division.

PFA APPEARANCES: 2

Dennis Bergkamp,
Arsenal

The Dutchman starred as the Gunners secured a domestic double. Scored 16 times in 28 games, including a fabulous hat-trick at Leicester. But his natural skill and ability to supply is what really stood out. The striker was also named PFA Player of the Year.

PFA APPEARANCES: 1

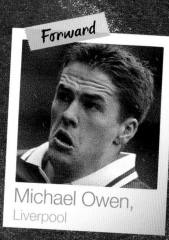

Michael Owen,
Liverpool

Liverpool's teen sensation was a constant menace throughout the season. The PFA Young Player of the Year's blistering pace and finishing ability saw him notch 18 goals in 36 league games – joint top scorer in the division. Owen made his England debut and was selected for the World Cup 1998 squad at the age of 18.

PFA APPEARANCES: 1

PFA TEAM OF THE YEAR 1998-1999

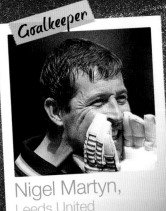

Goalkeeper

Nigel Martyn,
Leeds United

The England stopper made it two appearances in a row as he helped Leeds finish fourth. Was largely responsible for United's record of conceding just 34 goals all season – the third best in the division. Kept 13 clean sheets in his 34 starts throughout the campaign.

PFA APPEARANCES: 2

Defender

Gary Neville,
Manchester United

Selected for a fourth time after another top-class season, the England right back played a huge part in United claiming an historic treble. Played 32 times in the Premier League and scored a vital goal against Everton as the Red Devils finished a point ahead of Arsenal.

PFA APPEARANCES: 4

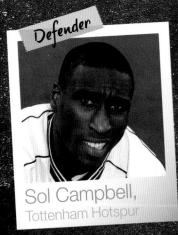

Defender

Sol Campbell,
Tottenham Hotspur

The England man carried on his good World Cup form with Spurs, missing just one of the season's 38 league games. Helped the North London side to 11th and the League Cup. Also scored six times, including a brace against Manchester United.

PFA APPEARANCES: 1

Defender

Jaap Stam,
Manchester United

The Dutchman showed why United had made him the most expensive defender in history at £10.6m, following a superb debut season. Played 54 games throughout the treble-winning campaign, making vital tackles and clearances. Scored his only goal in the 6-2 thrashing of Leicester City.

PFA APPEARANCES: 1

Defender

Denis Irwin,
Manchester United

Another consistent performer for United at the back, the Republic of Ireland full back was still proving a tough nut for wingers to crack even at 34 years of age. Scored vital goals in both games against Liverpool.

PFA APPEARANCES: 2

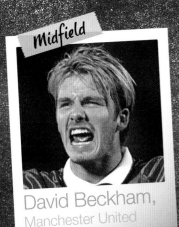

David Beckham,
Manchester United

The England midfielder bounced back from being sent off in the World Cup to have a fantastic campaign for United. Earned his third consecutive inclusion by setting up numerous goals from set pieces, and scored six himself. Struck vital goals against Villa and at home to Spurs to help his side win their seventh Premier League title.

PFA APPEARANCES: 3

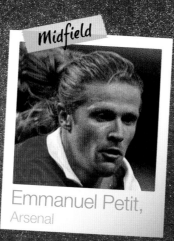

Emmanuel Petit,
Arsenal

Fresh from scoring in France's triumphant World Cup Final, the classy midfielder had another impressive season alongside Vieira at Arsenal. The 28-year-old was selected for the PFA side despite only making 27 league appearances. Scored four times, including the winner at Blackburn Rovers.

PFA APPEARANCES: 1

Patrick Vieira,
Arsenal

Although Arsenal fell just short of retaining the title, their skipper was in fine form once more, earning his first selection into the PFA XI. The France star was a dominant force in the middle of the park in most of his 34 league appearances. Scored three goals for the Gunners, including one in the 6-1 win at Middlesbrough.

PFA APPEARANCES: 1

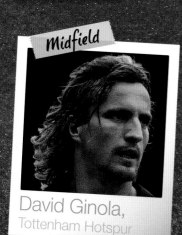

David Ginola,
Tottenham Hotspur

Despite playing in a side that finished mid-table, the France winger lit up White Hart Lane with performances full of flair and skill. Scored just three goals in 30 games but contributed to many more. Instrumental in helping Spurs win the League Cup.

PFA APPEARANCES: 2

Dwight Yorke,
Manchester United

The Trinidad and Tobago star was an instant hit at Old Trafford following his move from Aston Villa. Yorke was joint top scorer with 18 league goals as United collected three major trophies. Linked up brilliantly with fellow striker Andy Cole. Struck a hat-trick at Leicester and a winner at Middlesbrough.

PFA APPEARANCES: 1

Nicolas Anelka,
Arsenal

The French youngster wowed Highbury with his blistering speed and eye for goal. The striker's 17 league goals in 35 matches saw him collect the PFA Young Player of the Year Award in just his second full season in England. The 20-year-old made a £22.3m move to Real Madrid in summer 1999.

PFA APPEARANCES: 1

PFA TEAM OF THE YEAR 1999-2000

Goalkeeper

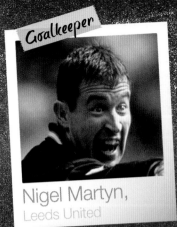

Nigel Martyn,
Leeds United

The Leeds United No.1 made it three consecutive appearances in the PFA XI after helping the club to a record high finish of third in the Premier League. The England keeper kept 13 clean sheets and was an ever-present as Leeds qualified for the Champions League for the first time. Part of the Three Lions' Euro 2000 squad.

PFA APPEARANCES: 3

Defender

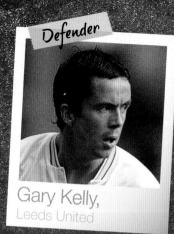

Gary Kelly,
Leeds United

The right back's second inclusion in the PFA selection came after another top year with the Elland Road outfit. Played 31 league matches and was a key team member as Leeds reached the semi-finals of the UEFA Cup.

PFA APPEARANCES: 2

Defender

Jaap Stam,
Manchester United

The Holland international made it two out of two after maintaining the form from his fantastic debut season at Old Trafford. A dominant figure at the heart of United's defence, Stam was feared by many centre forwards. Made 33 league appearances and helped the Red Devils claim a seventh Premier League title.

PFA APPEARANCES: 2

Defender

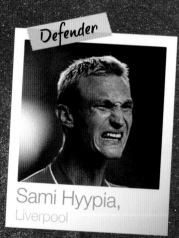

Sami Hyypia,
Liverpool

Was an ever-present in his first Premier League season. The Finland international proved to everyone that Liverpool had got a bargain at £2.6m. Dominant in the air and a good reader of the game, the 26-year-old scored twice and was a big reason why the Merseysiders had the best defence in the league, conceding just 30 times.

PFA APPEARANCES: 1

Defender

Ian Harte,
Leeds United

The Republic of Ireland full back earned a first selection to the PFA side with a string of first-class showings. Scored six goals in 33 league games as his wonderful ability from set pieces shone through. Hit vital winners against Spurs, West Ham, Bradford City and Derby, as Leeds claimed third by two points.

PFA APPEARANCES: 1

Midfield

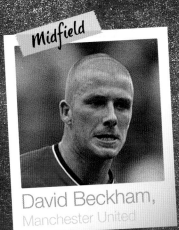

David Beckham,
Manchester United

The United midfielder played a major part in capturing his fourth Premier League title. The England man scored six times in 30 league matches, including the winner at Middlesbrough and one in the 7-1 thrashing of West Ham. Claimed the most assists with 17 and was part of the Three Lions' Euro 2000 squad.

PFA APPEARANCES: 4

Midfield

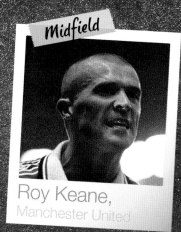

Roy Keane,
Manchester United

The Republic of Ireland skipper was named PFA Player of the Year for the first time after another impressive campaign. Led United to another title, excelling in both halves of the field. Scored 12 times — his best year in front of goal — including a winning brace against Arsenal.

PFA APPEARANCES: 3

Midfield

Patrick Vieira,
Arsenal

The France star starred again for Arsenal, powering his way through the season. Vieira was instrumental in taking the Gunners to the UEFA Cup Final and runner-up spot in the league. Scored twice and was included in France's Euro 2000 squad.

PFA APPEARANCES: 2

Midfield

Harry Kewell,
Leeds United

The Australian had his best year yet in a Leeds shirt and scored ten times in 36 league matches as United claimed third. Also notched five goals in a UEFA Cup campaign that ended in the semi-finals. The 21-year-old's technique and work ethic saw him named PFA Young Player of the Year.

PFA APPEARANCES: 1

Forward

Andrew Cole,
Manchester United

The England frontman struck another hat full of goals with 19 in 28 leagues appearances that helped fire the Red Devils to yet another title. Cole's strikes included four against former club Newcastle. But this still was not enough to earn a call up to his country's Euro 2000 squad.

PFA APPEARANCES: 1

Forward

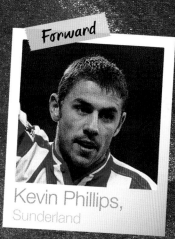

Kevin Phillips,
Sunderland

Sunderland's No.10 became just the third player to score 30 times in a Premier League season. The 26-year-old struck all different types of goals for the Black Cats who finished seventh. The striker became the first Englishman to win the European Golden Shoe and was rewarded with a call up to the Three Lions' Euro 2000 squad.

PFA APPEARANCES: 1

PFA TEAM OF THE YEAR 2000-2001

Fabien Barthez,
Manchester United

United paid £7.8m to sign World Cup-winning keeper Barthez – and the France star had a top first season at Old Trafford. Kept clean sheets in 15 of his 30 league appearances as the Red Devils conceded just 31 goals on the way to capturing a third title in a row.

PFA APPEARANCES: 1

Stephen Carr,
Tottenham Hotspur

Impressed in what was a mediocre year for Spurs, who finished 12th in the league. Ireland's right back scored three times in 28 appearances, including one in the opening day win over Ipswich. Very consistent and Tottenham won just twice in ten games without their talented No.2.

PFA APPEARANCES: 1

Jaap Stam,
Manchester United

The Holland defender kept up his perfect record of making the PFA XI since moving to United in 1998, despite turning out in just 15 league games. The 28-year-old was at his dominant best in those matches, and played a key role in securing a third consecutive title.

PFA APPEARANCES: 3

Wes Brown,
Manchester United

The 21-year-old showed what all the hype was about as he shone throughout his breakthrough season. The England central defender played 28 times as United cruised to the title. His ability both on and off the ball played a huge part in the Red Devils' impressive defensive record.

PFA APPEARANCES: 1

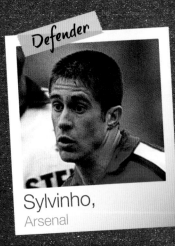

Sylvinho,
Arsenal

The Brazilian improved on his debut year performances and scored four times in 31 appearances, which included a fantastic late equaliser at Chelsea. Showed signs of defensive improvement but was a real outlet going forward, bombing up field in support of his team-mates whenever possible.

PFA APPEARANCES: 1

Midfield

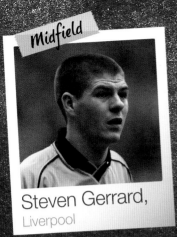

Steven Gerrard,
Liverpool

The 20-year-old had a magnificent third season in the Liverpool side. Played 41 times as the Reds won the League, FA and UEFA Cup treble. Scored nine goals, including one in the UEFA Final against Alaves and a thunderbolt in the win over Manchester United. Began to establish himself in the England team and was PFA Young Player of the Year.

PFA APPEARANCES: 1

Midfield

Roy Keane,
Manchester United

United's skipper was again in supreme form as he steered his side to the title. Scored twice in 28 league appearances, including one in the 6-1 mauling of Arsenal. The Irishman's enthusiasm, energy and ability proved why he was rated as one of the best midfielders in world football.

PFA APPEARANCES: 4

Midfield

Patrick Vieira,
Arsenal

Three in a row for the France star who carried the confidence gained by winning Euro 2000 over to the club season. Had his highest scoring campaign to date, netting six times in 30 league matches, including the winner at Southampton. A bright light in what was a trophyless season for the Gunners.

PFA APPEARANCES: 3

Midfield

Ryan Giggs,
Manchester United

United's flying winger was included for a third time in the PFA XI, eight years after his first selection in 1993. Scored seven times in 44 appearances as the Welshman and his club won a seventh Premier League. Linked well with the strikers throughout the season and supplied quality from the left flank.

PFA APPEARANCES: 3

Forward

Teddy Sheringham,
Manchester United

Collected the PFA Player of the Year award after playing some of the best football of his career at the age of 35. United's top scorer, with 21 goals in all competitions, the England striker hit a hat-trick against Southampton and braces against Bradford City and Leicester. Returned to Tottenham during the summer.

PFA APPEARANCES: 1

Forward

Thierry Henry,
Arsenal

After netting 17 Premier League goals during his debut season, Arsenal's No.14 replicated that form as his side finished second. Scored a stunning winner against Manchester United and a hat-trick against Leicester. The 23-year-old's pace and trickery made him incredibly hard to stop.

PFA APPEARANCES: 1

PFA TEAM OF THE YEAR 2001-2002

Goalkeeper

Shay Given,
Newcastle United

The super stopper was in top-class form once more for the Magpies. Played every Premier League game and kept nine clean sheets as Newcastle finished in the top four for the first time since 1997. The 26-year-old's form saw him selected as Ireland's No.1 for the 2002 World Cup.

PFA APPEARANCES: 1

Defender

Steve Finnan,
Fulham

The right back completed his rise from non league by being among the country's best XI. Was a key member of the Fulham side that finished a creditable 13th in their debut Premier League season. An ever-present who was a reliable and solid performer that no winger liked to face. Included in Ireland's 2002 World Cup squad.

PFA APPEARANCES: 1

Defender

Rio Ferdinand,
Leeds United

The young England star was included for the first time as he moved up another level with Leeds. Played 31 times in the league and helped United to the third-best defensive record and fifth. His calmness, vision and ability to distribute from the back earned him a place in England's World Cup squad. Sold to Man United for a record-breaking £30m in summer 2002.

PFA APPEARANCES: 1

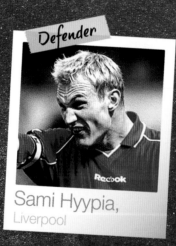

Defender

Sami Hyypia,
Liverpool

The Finn was selected for the second time in three seasons after helping the Reds claim second place – their highest finish in the Premier League. The central defender was the main reason his side had the best defensive record having conceded just 30 times. Chipped in with three goals in matches that all ended in victories.

PFA APPEARANCES: 2

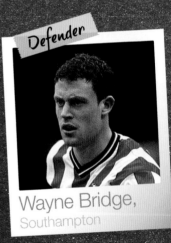

Defender

Wayne Bridge,
Southampton

The first Southampton player to make the PFA XI since Matt Le Tissier in 1995, the left back was an ever-present for Saints for a second consecutive campaign. Failed to score but showed great quality and desire down the left. Southampton's 11th place finish had a lot to do with the consistency of Bridge. Made his England debut in February and played at the 2002 World Cup.

PFA APPEARANCES: 1

Midfield

Robert Pires,
Arsenal

Arsenal's No.7 was selected despite missing the final month of the season with a cruciate ligament injury. The Frenchman scored nine goals in 28 league matches, including the opener at rivals Tottenham. Showed his flair and magic, often linking up with Henry as he secured his first trophies since his move to England.

PFA APPEARANCES: 1

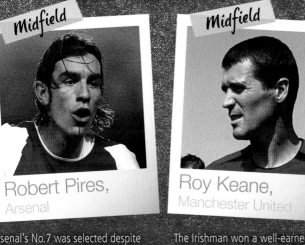

Midfield

Roy Keane,
Manchester United

The Irishman won a well-earned fifth inclusion in the Team of the Year. Played 44 games in all competitions as he skippered United to third. Keano shone in a disappointing season for his club as he scored three times and led by example. Included in Ireland's squad for World Cup 2002.

PFA APPEARANCES: 5

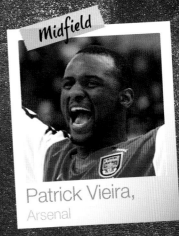

Midfield

Patrick Vieira,
Arsenal

Arsenal's midfield general drove the club to a second domestic double in five seasons. Scored three goals in 28 appearances, including strikes in the wins against Aston Villa and Fulham. Was a dominant force in the FA Cup Final and was selected for the 2002 World Cup by France.

PFA APPEARANCES: 4

Midfield

Ryan Giggs,
Manchester United

The Welshman produced another high quality, consistent season at Old Trafford. Scored seven times in 25 league appearances, including a brace in the win at Fulham. Laid on two goals on for the Reds' win at Chelsea. A constant menace down the left, always seeking to attack the opposing right back.

PFA APPEARANCES: 4

Forward

Ruud van Nistelrooy,
Manchester United

The Holland star showed why United had paid £19m for his signature despite a serious injury the previous year. He netted 36 times during his debut season, with 23 league goals that included a hat-trick against Southampton. Constantly in the right place at the right time and also named the PFA Player of the Year.

PFA APPEARANCES: 1

Forward

Thierry Henry,
Arsenal

The Gunners' No.14 struck more than 30 goals for the first time in his career as he fired the club to a domestic double. Won the Golden Boot with 24 league strikes, including seven braces. Selected for France's 2002 World Cup squad.

PFA APPEARANCES: 2

PFA TEAM OF THE YEAR 2002-2003

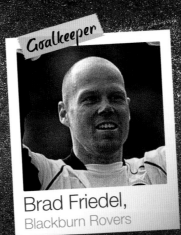

Goalkeeper

Brad Friedel,
Blackburn Rovers

The USA shot-stopper kept an impressive 15 clean sheets in 37 league matches for Rovers. Conceded just 40 times, which was a very good record for a side that crept into the top-six.

PFA APPEARANCES: 1

Defender

Stephen Carr,
Tottenham Hotspur

The Irishman made the PFA XI for the second time in three years after further impressive showings for Spurs. The club finished 11th but the right back shone in the majority of his 30 league games. Carr's raiding runs and eye for a tackle made him a tough nut to crack.

PFA APPEARANCES: 2

Defender

Sol Campbell,
Arsenal

The powerful centre back carried his decent World Cup performances into the season with Arsenal. Scored two goals in 33 league matches but impressed in stopping opposing strikers. Helped the Gunners finish second and keep nine clean sheets. Missed the FA Cup Final victory through injury.

PFA APPEARANCES: 2

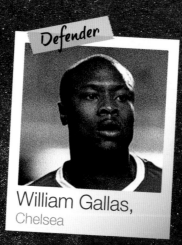

Defender

William Gallas,
Chelsea

The newly capped France international improved on his debut season performances at Chelsea. The 23-year-old's defensive abilities and four vital goals helped the Blues creep into the top-four on the final day of the season. An ever-present for Claudio Ranieri's side that had the second best defensive record having conceded just 38 times.

PFA APPEARANCES: 1

Defender

Ashley Cole,
Arsenal

The highly-rated left back made 41 appearances in all competitions and scored once in a win at West Brom. Helped the Gunners keep a clean sheet and retain the FA Cup in a 1-0 win over Southampton in Cardiff.

PFA APPEARANCES: 1

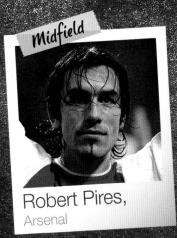

Midfield

Robert Pires,
Arsenal

The 29-year-old playmaker showed his stunning second season had been no fluke by bettering his stats this time round. He missed the first couple of months of the campaign as he recovered from a cruciate ligament injury but then scored 19 goals in 46 games, including the FA Cup Final winner.

PFA APPEARANCES: 2

Midfield

Paul Scholes,
Manchester United

The only title-winner in the Team of the Year, and his first inclusion, the England star collected his sixth Premier League medal after hitting 14 goals in 33 league matches. Scored two braces against Blackburn and a stunning hat-trick in the 6-2 win at Newcastle. Assisted with eight more goals.

PFA APPEARANCES: 1

Midfield

Patrick Vieira,
Arsenal

The newly appointed Arsenal captain was one of the best midfielders in the league for a fifth year running, despite playing just 24 league games. Scored three goals, all resulting in victories, and made a huge contribution to the club's victorious FA Cup run.

PFA APPEARANCES: 5

Midfield

Kieron Dyer,
Newcastle United

The 24-year-old had his best and most consistent season to date. Played 35 league games and scored a winning brace at Leeds. The England man's pace, trickery and movement were a constant threat and heavily contributed to the Magpies qualifying for the Champions League.

PFA APPEARANCES: 1

Forward

Alan Shearer,
Newcastle United

The former England captain was included for the first time since 2007 after another productive year for Newcastle. Scored 23 times in all competitions, including three braces and a stunning winner against Everton. The No.9's form helped the Magpies achieve another third place finish.

PFA APPEARANCES: 7

Forward

Thierry Henry,
Arsenal

The France forward collected his first PFA Player of the Year Award after a fantastic campaign. The league's second-top scorer with 24 in 37 matches, which included a brace against Manchester United. Helped the Gunners win the FA Cup for the second consecutive year and was the top assister, creating 23 goals.

PFA APPEARANCES: 3

PFA TEAM OF THE YEAR 2003-2004

Goalkeeper

Tim Howard,
Manchester United

The American was an unknown quantity following his move from MetroStars but that all changed after his debut season at Old Trafford. Howard suffered a few shaky moments but also made a host of world-class saves. Collected 12 clean sheets in 32 league games and won the FA Cup.

PFA APPEARANCES: 1

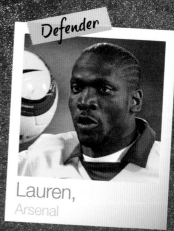

Defender

Lauren,
Arsenal

The Cameroon international had by far his best season at Highbury, defensively sound and was a great outlet going forward. Didn't score but began many moves that resulted in goals. Played 32 league games as Arsenal went the season unbeaten to be Christened 'The Invincibles'.

PFA APPEARANCES: 1

Defender

Sol Campbell,
Arsenal

Another 'Invincible', the England defender had a dominant third season for the Gunners. Played 35 times and scored in the 2-0 win over Aston Villa. Made numerous vital challenges that played a big part in Arsenal's stunning and historic record. His form earned a call up to the England's Euro 2004 squad.

PFA APPEARANCES: 3

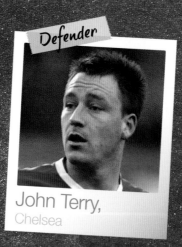

Defender

John Terry,
Chelsea

The newly capped England centre half gained confidence from making his international debut in June 2003. Played 50 times in all competitions and scored two league goals, as the Blues finished second after Roman Abtramovich's first season as owner. Wore his heart on his sleeve, made tackles that many would think twice about. Selected for his first major tournament, Euro 2004.

PFA APPEARANCES: 1

Defender

Ashley Cole,
Arsenal

After breaking into the side the previous year, the 23-year-old had established himself as Arsenal and England's first choice left back. Played 31 league games as the Gunners went the season unbeaten. His defensive side improved with each game and he was also comfortable attacking. Went to Euro 2004 with the Three Lions.

PFA APPEARANCES: 2

Midfield

Steven Gerrard,
Liverpool

The midfielder was the shining light in what was a disappointing season for Liverpool. Scored four times in 34 league games, including a stunning winner against Manchester City. Led by example once again and was selected for England's Euro 2004 squad.

PFA APPEARANCES: 2

Midfield

Frank Lampard,
Chelsea

Earned his first selection into the PFA XI after his goal scoring reached double-figures for the first time in his career. An ever-present during a season when he made his Champions League debut. Hit braces in the wins over Blackburn and Southampton and laid on five assists. Included in England's Euro 2004 squad.

PFA APPEARANCES: 1

Midfield

Patrick Vieira,
Arsenal

Skipper of the 'Invincibles', the France star was included for a sixth consecutive season as he again dominate the midfield. Scored three goals in 29 league matches, including one as the Gunners wrapped up the title at rivals Spurs. Vieira's power and class were simply outstanding. The 27-year-old was picked by France for Euro 2004.

PFA APPEARANCES: 6

Midfield

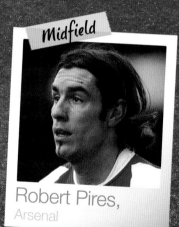

Robert Pires,
Arsenal

Henry scored most of the goals but his fellow Frenchman was one of the most consistent performers. Scored 14 times and assisted with five goals in 36 league appearances. Struck vital goals against Liverpool and was on the score sheet when the Gunners clinched the title at Tottenham. His touch, skill and poise on the ball is something that's rarely seen.

PFA APPEARANCES: 3

Forward

Ruud van Nistelrooy,
Manchester United

The Dutchman showed off his fantastic finishing ability once more by bagging 20 league goals and 37 in all competitions. Struck a brace in United's triumphant FA Cup Final. Selected in Holland's Euro 2004 squad – his first major international tournament.

PFA APPEARANCES: 2

Forward

Thierry Henry,
Arsenal

The France forward was unstoppable as the Gunners went through the league season unbeaten. Collected the Golden Boot that he'd missed out on the previous year by hitting 30 goals in 37 league matches, including a hat-trick against Liverpool and four at home to Leeds. Included in France's Euro 2004 squad.

PFA APPEARANCES: 4

PFA TEAM OF THE YEAR 2004–2005

Goalkeeper
Petr Cech,
Chelsea

The giant shot-stopper was superb in his debut season at Stamford Bridge, as Chelsea won their first title for 50 years. Replaced Carlo Cudicini as the club's No.1 and went a then Premier League record of 1,025 minutes without conceding. Kept a record 21 clean sheets and conceded just 15 times in England's elite division, another best.

PFA APPEARANCES: 1

Defender
Gary Neville,
Manchester United

The England man made the PFA XI for the first time since 1999, as he appeared to improve with age. At the age of 30, the Red Devils' stalwart played 22 league games and collected two assists. In a trophyless campaign for the club, Neville's performances were a highlight.

PFA APPEARANCES: 5

Defender
Rio Ferdinand,
Manchester United

United's star centre back impressed after returning from an eight-month ban for missing a drugs test. Played 31 league games, in which the Red Devils conceded just 21 times. United could only finish third despite going unbeaten for 20 matches.

PFA APPEARANCES: 2

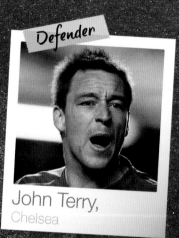

Defender
John Terry,
Chelsea

The 24-year-old was made club captain by new boss Jose Mourinho and guided the Blues to a first title since 1954. Played 36 times in the league and scored an important goal in the draw at Arsenal. Steered Chelsea to League Cup glory and was the main man in a record-breaking defence. The PFA Player of the Year.

PFA APPEARANCES: 1

Defender
Ashley Cole,
Arsenal

The Gunners' left back had quickly established himself as one of the best defenders in Europe and boosted his reputation by earning a third successive inclusion in the PFA XI. Played 35 league games and scored in wins at Man City and Aston Villa. Successful in the FA Cup Final shoot-out against Man United.

PFA APPEARANCES: 3

Midfield

Steven Gerrard,
Liverpool

The Liverpool star inspired an amazing comeback in the Champions League Final against AC Milan. Scored 13 goals in all competitions as the Reds had to settle for fifth in the league. Named UEFA Club Footballer of the Year.

PFA APPEARANCES: 3

Midfield

Frank Lampard,
Chelsea

The England star again took his game to a new level and scored 24 goals in all competitions, as Chelsea won a Premier League and League Cup double. Struck 13 times in the top-flight and was the highest assister with 16. Hit a winning brace at Bolton as the title was sealed by the Blues.

PFA APPEARANCES: 2

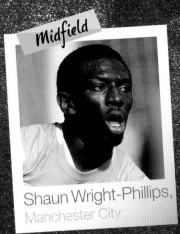

Midfield

Shaun Wright-Phillips,
Manchester City

The 23-year-old lit up the City of Manchester Stadium with displays of top-class skill. Played 33 league games and scored 11 times, including a stunning equaliser in the draw at Arsenal. Helped the club finish eighth and earned his first England call up in August. Bought by Chelsea for £21m.

PFA APPEARANCES: 1

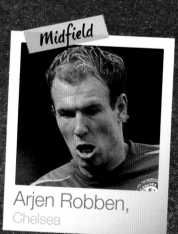

Midfield

Arjen Robben,
Chelsea

Missed the start of Chelsea's title-winning campaign through injury, but the Holland star demonstrated why the Blues spent £12m to buy him. Scored seven goals in 18 league matches, including winners against Everton and Blackburn, and produced nine assists. The winger's blistering pace and quick feet had many full backs in knots.

PFA APPEARANCES: 1

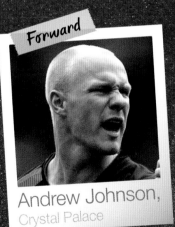

Forward

Andrew Johnson,
Crystal Palace

The Eagles' hitman took the league by storm on the South Londoners return to the top-flight. Scored 21 of the club's 41 goals, including a Premier League record eight penalties, which led to a first England call up. Despite his impressive strike rate, Palace failed to survive.

PFA APPEARANCES: 1

Forward

Thierry Henry,
Arsenal

Arsenal's main man was selected for a fifth consecutive year after another goal-crazy season. Hit the net 25 times in just 32 league appearances to win the Golden Boot for the third time in four years. Contributed the second most assists in the division with 14. A joy to watch for fans but a nightmare for opposing defenders.

PFA APPEARANCES: 5

PFA TEAM OF THE YEAR 2005-2006

Goalkeeper

Shay Given,
Newcastle United

The Republic of Ireland's No.1 was again in fine form throughout his eleventh season at Newcastle. An ever-present between the sticks, Given kept 13 clean sheets, including one at home to champions Chelsea, as the Magpies finished seventh.

PFA APPEARANCES: 2

Defender

Pascal Chimbonda,
Wigan Athletic

The full back starred in the Latics' first season in the Premier League when he played 37 times. Scored the winner at home to Fulham and showed defensive qualities which saw Wigan finish 10th and reach the League Cup Final. Called up to France's 2006 World Cup squad.

PFA APPEARANCES: 1

Defender

Jamie Carragher,
Liverpool

The Reds stalwart was included in the PFA XI for the first time after yet another fantastic season. The 28-year-old played 36 league games in a defence that conceded just 25 times – the second-best in the division. Played 63 times in all competitions, won the FA Cup and his consistency earned him a place in England's 2006 World Cup squad.

PFA APPEARANCES: 1

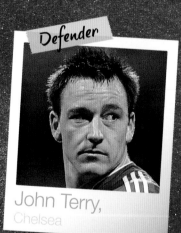

Defender

John Terry,
Chelsea

The Chelsea captain continued his rise to becoming one of the best defenders in the country, as he led the Blues to back-to-back titles. The 25-year-old helped the club win 15 of their first 16 games and concede just 22 times all season. Notched vital winners against Middlesbrough and West Brom. Rewarded with a spot in the England squad for the World Cup finals.

PFA APPEARANCES: 2

Defender

William Gallas,
Chelsea

Gallas proved his class in a number of positions. Deployed at centre back and the unfamiliar role of left back during a campaign in which he played 34 times in the league, providing two goals and scoring five, including a last-minute winner against Tottenham. Went to the World Cup finals with France before joining Arsenal.

PFA APPEARANCES: 2

Midfield

Steven Gerrard,
Liverpool

The Liverpool skipper collected the PFA Player of the Year award for the first time after another season of brilliance. Scored 20 goals in all competitions, including a brace in the FA Cup Final win over West Ham. The England man's shooting from long range, eye for a pass and leadership skills helped the Reds to third in the league. The 25-year-old then went to the World Cup finals.

PFA APPEARANCES: 4

Midfield

Frank Lampard,
Chelsea

Chelsea's No.8 made it a third consecutive inclusion in the PFA XI after another progressive year for the Blues. Scored 16 league goals and 21 times in all competitions as the side defended the title. Also contributed with eight assists. His form saw him selected for a first World Cup finals with England.

PFA APPEARANCES: 3

Midfield

Cristiano Ronaldo,
Manchester United

The Portugal youngster came of age at Old Trafford after a couple of seasons finding his feet. Scored nine times in 33 league games, including three braces. Produced seven assists for his team-mates and struck in United's League Cup Final win over Wigan. The 21-year-old's skills and pace were a joy to watch.

PFA APPEARANCES: 1

Midfield

Joe Cole,
Chelsea

The Chelsea playmaker produced moments of magic throughout the season. Scored 13 times in all competitions, including a fantastic solo goal against Manchester United on the day the Blues retained the title. Credited with six assists despite having to adapt to playing across the midfield. Went to World Cup finals with England.

PFA APPEARANCES: 1

Forward

Wayne Rooney,
Manchester United

England's main man scored 16 goals in 36 league games, form that saw him retain the PFA Young Player of the Year award. Created nine goals for United, who had to settle for second behind Chelsea. Struck a brace as United won the League Cup Final and was selected for his first World Cup, aged 20.

PFA APPEARANCES: 1

Forward

Thierry Henry,
Arsenal

Arsenal's star striker secured the Golden Boot for the third season running and fourth time in five years after hitting 27 goals in 32 games. The France star became the Gunners' record goalscorer and scored two hat-tricks, including one in the final game at Highbury against Wigan. Selected for a fifth consecutive major tournament by his country.

PFA APPEARANCES: 6

PFA TEAM OF THE YEAR 2006-2007

Goalkeeper

Edwin van der Sar,
Manchester United

The Holland shot-stopper made his first appearance in the PFA side after United won the title for the first time since 2003. The keeper played 32 times in a Red Devils team that conceded just 27 times. Saved a penalty to help his side win the Manchester derby — and were crowned champions the following day in May.

PFA APPEARANCES: 1

Defender

Gary Neville,
Manchester United

The 32-year-old defied his age and gained a sixth entry into the PFA team after producing one of his best-ever seasons in a United shirt. His rampaging runs and defensive experience was invaluable to the club in his 24 league matches. Neville was also England boss Steve McClaren's undisputed first choice at right back.

PFA APPEARANCES: 6

Defender

Rio Ferdinand,
Manchester United

Ferdinand made his third appearance in the PFA listings after a terrific season alongside Nemanja Vidic at the heart of the Man United defence. Played 33 times and scored one goal in the vital 2-0 win against rivals Liverpool.

PFA APPEARANCES: 3

Defender

Nemanja Vidic,
Manchester United

Ferdinand's partner was a rock all season, earning him his first introduction into the PFA side. Scored three times and was dominant in both boxes with his athleticism and heading ability often getting the better of opposing strikers.

PFA APPEARANCES: 1

Defender

Patrice Evra,
Manchester United

The Frenchman made it an all-United back five in the PFA selections as he was included for the first time. Played just 24 games, but was impressive in both defence and attacking roles. Scored once in the 3-0 win over Everton.

PFA APPEARANCES: 1

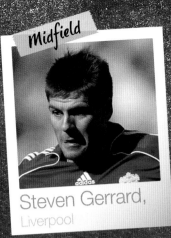

Midfield

Steven Gerrard,
Liverpool

The England star missed just two league matches as he guided Liverpool to third. Gerrard was as creative as ever to claim a place in the PFA's best XI for the fifth time. Scored seven league goals, including the winner against Manchester City.

PFA APPEARANCES: 5

Midfield

Paul Scholes,
Manchester United

Surprisingly this was only the second selection for Scholes in the PFA XI. His six goals in 30 games played a major part in United capturing their ninth Premier League crown. Hit vital strikes against Liverpool, Newcastle and Blackburn. Scholes' expert range of passing also set up numerous goal scoring opportunities.

PFA APPEARANCES: 2

Midfield

Cristiano Ronaldo,
Manchester United

The United winger became only the second player to collect both the PFA Player and Young Player of the Year awards after a fantastic season. The Portugal international was the league's third-top scorer with 17 goals and joint-top assister with 13. Missed just four league games this season.

PFA APPEARANCES: 2

Midfield

Ryan Giggs,
Manchester United

The Welshman was selected by PFA members for a fifth time after helping United clinch the title for the first time in four years. The 33-year-old played 30 league games and scored four goals. He hit the winner against Spurs, and notched vital strikes at Watford and Fulham. Also won nine assists.

PFA APPEARANCES: 5

Forward

Didier Drogba,
Chelsea

The league's Golden Boot winner with 20 goals, the Ivor Coast striker had his best season to date in a Chelsea shirt. Some of those goals came in important games against the likes of Newcastle, Everton and Liverpool but it wasn't enough to clinch a third consecutive title for Chelsea.

PFA APPEARANCES: 1

Forward

Dimitar Berbatov,
Tottenham Hotspur

Made the PFA best XI afer his first season in England. The Bulgarian lit up White Hart Lane with a number of stunning performances. Scored 12 goals, including one in the North London derby, and assisted a further 11 for his team-mates. Proved a great addition to the Premier League.

PFA APPEARANCES: 1

PFA TEAM OF THE YEAR 2007-2008

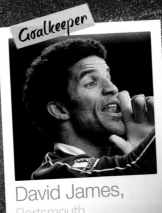

Goalkeeper

David James,
Portsmouth

Jamo broke a Premier League record by claiming his 142nd clean sheet in a goalless draw with Aston Villa. Played 35 times during his second season with Pompey and kept 17 clean sheets. Also became the third player to cross the 500-game mark in England's elite league.

PFA APPEARANCES: 2

Defender

Bacary Sagna,
Arsenal

In his debut season with Arsenal the full back played 29 league games, claimed four assists and scored once. The Frenchman's ability in both defence and attack was clear to see and his direct, lung-busting runs helped the Gunners take the game to the opposition. His form earned a regular spot in the France national team.

PFA APPEARANCES: 1

Defender

Rio Ferdinand,
Manchester United

Ferdinand was included for the fourth time and his third appearance in the PFA side in four years after again impressing in the Red Devils' backline. Helped United to claim the title with 21 clean sheets, joint best with Chelsea. Scored twice, including one in the 6-0 thrashing of Newcastle.

PFA APPEARANCES: 4

Defender

Nemanja Vidic,
Manchester United

The Serbian was selected alongside team-mate Ferdinand again after helping United concede just 22 goals all season. Played 32 times and scored a vital winner at Everton in September. Made countless defensive clearances and telling tackles that contributed towards United's triumph.

PFA APPEARANCES: 2

Defender

Gael Clichy,
Arsenal

The Frenchman's inclusion meant Arsenal filled both full back spots. An ever-present at left back, he raided forward at any opportunity. His attacking midset led to six assists, while his tenacity saw the North London side concede just 31 goals, the fourth best in the league.

PFA APPEARANCES: 1

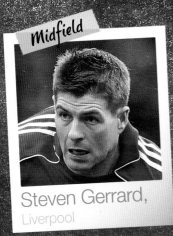

Midfield

Steven Gerrard,
Liverpool

Mr Liverpool was selected for a fifth consecutive year after his tenth senior season with his boyhood club. Scored 11 times in 34 league games, and created chance after chance for his team-mates. Made his 300th Premier League appearance in the Reds midfield against Blackburn Rovers in April.

PFA APPEARANCES: 6

Midfield

Cesc Fabregas,
Arsenal

Was a class apart in the Gunners midfield. Created 19 goals, the most in the league, and scored seven times, including strikes against Tottenham, Liverpool and Manchester United. Named PFA Young Player of the Year as Arsenal came close to lifting the title for the first time since 2004.

PFA APPEARANCES: 1

Midfield

Cristiano Ronaldo,
Manchester United

PFA Player of the Year for the second year in a row following an unbelievable campaign. Golden Boot winner after crashing home 31 goals in 34 games, including strikers against title rivals Chelsea, Arsenal and Liverpool. The Portugal star's total made him just the fifth player to score 30-plus times in one Premier League season.

PFA APPEARANCES: 2

Midfield

Ashley Young,
Aston Villa

Shone during his first full season as a Villan, as he caused problems for opposing full backs. Scored eight goals and collected a remarkable 17 assists – the division's second highest – as Villa finished sixth, their highest finish since 2004. Young's form earned him his first England cap in November 2007.

PFA APPEARANCES: 1

Forward

Emmanuel Adebayor,
Arsenal

Stepped up to the plate in his second full season at Arsenal and scored 24 times in 36 league games. Hit two hat-tricks against rivals Tottenham, as the Gunners finished third, four points behind champions Manchester United. The Togo star's power in the air and on the ground was a nightmare for defenders.

PFA APPEARANCES: 1

Forward

Fernando Torres,
Liverpool

Set the Premier League alight during his first season and scored 24 times in 33 games. Notched against Chelsea, Manchester City, Arsenal and Tottenham. His movement, acceleration and deadly finishing made him an instant hit with the Anfield faithful. The Spaniard's goal tally was bettered only by Ronaldo.

PFA APPEARANCES: 1

PFA TEAM OF THE YEAR 2008-2009

Goalkeeper

Edwin van der Sar,
Manchester United

Included in the PFA list for the second time in three seasons after setting a Premier League record for minutes played without conceding. The Dutchman kept an amazing 14 clean sheets in a row and 21 in total. Played 33 league games, conceding just 20 goals, as United beat Liverpool to the title by four points.

PFA APPEARANCES: 2

Defender

Glen Johnson,
Portsmouth

Impressed for Pompey throughout the campaign and scoring three times in 29 appearances. Johnson's rampaging runs from full back caused opposition left backs all kinds of problems as the South Coast outfit finished a comfortable fourteenth.

PFA APPEARANCES: 1

Defender

Rio Ferdinand,
Manchester United

One half of United's formidable centre back partnership, the England man was as classy as ever in a season where United kept 24 clean sheets. Played 24 league matches in which the team conceded just 18 goals. Failed to score but set up a number of attacks by bringing the ball out from the back.

PFA APPEARANCES: 5

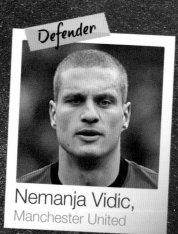

Defender

Nemanja Vidic,
Manchester United

Ferdinand's steely partner was included for the third season in a row after a string of world-class performances in United's backline. The Serbia star did whatever it took to keep the ball out, resulting in the Red Devils' impressive defensive record of 24 goals conceded. Played 34 league matches and scored four times, including the winner against Sunderland and a vital strike against Chelsea.

PFA APPEARANCES: 3

Defender

Patrice Evra,
Manchester United

The Frenchman's inclusion meant four of the back five came from United's record-breaking squad. Evra's second inclusion came following a season which saw him give opposing wingers a torrid time, consistently putting them on the back foot with his direct, clever and skilful runs into the attacking third. Improvemed defensively in his 28 league appearances, with well-timed challenges.

PFA APPEARANCES: 2

Midfield

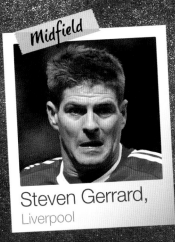

Steven Gerrard,
Liverpool

A sixth consecutive inclusion in the team of the year, during which the Anfield skipper recorded his highest Premier League tally of 16 goals. That included a hat-trick against Aston Villa and one at Man United. Also collected ten assists as the Reds came closer than ever to securing their first top-flight title since 1990.

PFA APPEARANCES: 7

Midfield

Ryan Giggs,
Manchester United

Made an incredible sixth appearance in the PFA list after his 19th season in a United shirt. Played 28 times and scored twice, including an important winner at West Ham. Played his 800th senior match against Arsenal in April. Used wide and in the centre of midfield. Named PFA Player of the Year for the first time.

PFA APPEARANCES: 6

Midfield

Cristiano Ronaldo,
Manchester United

The unmistakable talent of Ronaldo picked up where he'd left off the previous two years as he scored 18 goals in 33 league games, including important strikes against Aston Villa and Manchester City. Second-top scorer behind Nicolas Anelka, despite playing out wide. Ronaldo's pace, skill and athletism consistently kept fans entertained.

PFA APPEARANCES: 4

Midfield

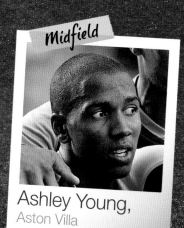

Ashley Young,
Aston Villa

The PFA Young Player of the Year dazzled defenders with his direct running and trickery and set up nine goals during a league campaign that saw Villa finish sixth. Scored eight times, largely through some wonderful free-kicks. Played 36 games and would've been an ever-present but for a suspension.

PFA APPEARANCES: 2

Forward

Nicolas Anelka,
Chelsea

Impressed in his first full season at Stamford Bridge as he was crowned top goalscorer with 19 goals in 37 games. Netted a hat-trick in the 5-0 demolition of Sunderland and his form kept Didier Drogba on the bench. The Frenchman had last been selected for the PFA team in 1999, during his short spell at Arsenal.

PFA APPEARANCES: 2

Forward

Fernando Torres,
Liverpool

Drafted in to the PFA for a second year running despite playing just 24 times. The Spain star notched 14 goals in those appearances, the most productive strike rate in the league. Scored both goals in the Merseyside derby win at Everton, two at Manchester City and two against Chelsea, as the Reds came just four points short of clinching the title.

PFA APPEARANCES: 2

PFA TEAM OF THE YEAR 2009-2010

Joe Hart,
Birmingham City

Made his first appearance in the PFA list following a successful loan spell at Birmingham City. Played 37 times for a side that conceded 47 goals and finished ninth, the Blues' highest finish for 51 years. Kept ten clean sheets during the campaign, made his England debut and broke into the Three Lions' World Cup squad.

PFA APPEARANCES: 1

Defender

Branislav Ivanovic,
Chelsea

Established himself as a key player in Chelsea's defence for the first time since his move from Lokomotiv Moscow. Played 29 league games, as the Blues won their third Premier League title and first since 2006. The side conceded just 26 goals in these matches.

PFA APPEARANCES: 1

Defender

Thomas Vermaelen,
Arsenal

The Belgium international was effective at both ends throughout the campaign. Played 33 league games and Arsenal conceded 34 times in those matches as they finished third. The centre back also scored seven times, including vital goals against Bolton and Stoke City.

PFA APPEARANCES: 1

Defender

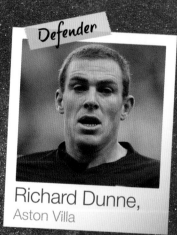

Richard Dunne,
Aston Villa

The Irishman was an ever-present for Villa, playing all 38 matches. Made numerous last-ditch challenges and clearances as the Villans secured sixth place. Played a major part in helping the club to the fourth-best defensive record this season, with just 39 goals conceded. Also got on the scoresheet three times, including goals against Manchester City and Chelsea.

PFA APPEARANCES: 1

Defender

Patrice Evra,
Manchester United

United's left back was selected for a second time after a thoroughly impressive campaign. Didn't miss a league match in a defence that kept 19 clean sheets, the most in the division. Conceded the least goals with 28 but missed out on the title to Chelsea by one point.

PFA APPEARANCES: 2

Midfield

Antonio Valencia,
Manchester United

Settled into life at Old Trafford quickly following his £16m switch from Wigan. Made 34 league appearances, scored five times and assisted in seven. Troubled full backs with his direct running and power that created space for his team-mates to exploit.

PFA APPEARANCES: 1

Midfield

Cesc Fabregas,
Arsenal

Dominated the majority of the 27 league games he played. Fabregas had his best goalscoring season and hit the net 15 times, including strikes against Tottenham, Aston Villa and Everton. Created 15 goals for his team-mates as the Gunners hit 83 league goals.

PFA APPEARANCES: 2

Midfield

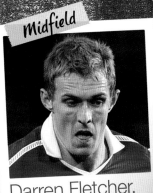

Darren Fletcher,
Manchester United

Enjoyed his best season in a United shirt. Played 30 league matches, assisted five goals and scored four times, including two in the 4-3 win over Man City. Noted for his energy and ability to read a game, allowing his more flamboyant team-mates to strike the killer blows.

PFA APPEARANCES: 1

Midfield

James Milner,
Aston Villa

The PFA Young Player of the Year had an extraordinary season for Villa. He was shifted into the heart of midfield to fill the void left by Gareth Barry and proved a worthy replacement. Scored seven times in 36 appearances, including the winner against rivals Birmingham City. Also collected 12 assists, contributing towards Villa's top six finish.

PFA APPEARANCES: 1

Forward

Wayne Rooney,
Manchester United

Included for a second time after producing his best goalscoring season in a United shirt. He netted 26 times in 32 games, a record only bettered by Didier Drogba. Scored two hat-tricks, which included a four-goal haul against Hull. His clinical performances saw him named PFA Player of the Year for the first time.

PFA APPEARANCES: 2

Forward

Didier Drogba,
Chelsea

The Premier League's top scorer with 29 goals in 32 games, his highest career tally. Drogba also claimed 13 assists, giving him a contribution to 42 of the Blues' 103 goals – a Premier League record. Scored a hat-trick in the 8-0 demolition of Wigan and strikes against Man United and Arsenal.

PFA APPEARANCES: 2

PFA TEAM OF THE YEAR 2010-2011

Goalkeeper

Edwin van der Sar,
Manchester United

Steered United to their 19th title with a string of world-class performances. Kept 15 clean sheets in 33 games, conceding just 31 times. Retired at the end of the season having won eight major trophies at Old Trafford.

PFA APPEARANCES: 3

Defender

Bacary Sagna,
Arsenal

The France international had arguably his best campaign in an Arsenal shirt, despite the club going a sixth season without a trophy. His rampaging runs from right back caused the opposition many problems. Scored one goal in 33 games and claimed three assists.

PFA APPEARANCES: 2

Defender

Nemanja Vidic,
Manchester United

Vidic was once again a rock at the heart of the United defence and fully deserved his place in the league's best XI for the fourth time in five years. Played 35 of the 38 league games, during which the team conceded 35 times. The captain scored five goals, including vital ones against Aston Villa, Tottenham and Chelsea.

PFA APPEARANCES: 4

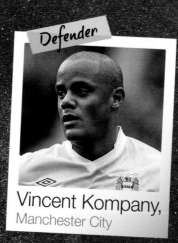

Defender

Vincent Kompany,
Manchester City

The Belgian established himself as City's top centre back during the campaign. Guided the club to a Premier League high finish of third to secure Champions League qualification for the first time in their history. Played all but one of the 38 league games which saw Roberto Mancini's side concede just 21 times – second best behind Chelsea with 20.

PFA APPEARANCES: 1

Defender

Ashley Cole,
Chelsea

The England left-back was included in the PFA roll call for the fourth time after appearing in all of Chelsea's 38 league matches. Helped the Blues concede just 33 goals, the joint lowest alongside Man City. Chelsea were runners-up as Cole assisted four goals. Still classy despite reaching the age of 30 years during the season.

PFA APPEARANCES: 4

Midfield

Nani,
Manchester United

By far the Portugal winger's best year in a Manchester United shirt. Finished top of the assists chart with 18 and scored nine himself as United secored 78 goals. Played 33 league matches, dazzling defenders with his skill and much-improved decision making.

PFA APPEARANCES: 1

Midfield

Samir Nasri,
Arsenal

Nasri was a bright spark in what was to be another trophyless season for the Gunners. Scored ten and assisted with one as Arsène Wenger guided his men to the fourth and final Champions League spot. Nasri hit goals against Tottenham and fellow top-four chasers Manchester City.

PFA APPEARANCES: 1

Midfield

Jack Wilshere,
Arsenal

The 18-year-old established himself in the Arsenal midfield and became PFA Young Player of the Year. Played 35 games and impressed with his energy, skill and intelligence. Scored his first Gunners league goal against Aston Villa and assisted three others as Arsenal finished fourth. Broke into the England side during the campaign.

PFA APPEARANCES: 1

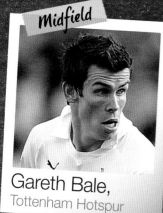

Midfield

Gareth Bale,
Tottenham Hotspur

The Welshman came of age in his fourth season at White Hart Lane. Scored seven league goals in 30 appearances but troubled defenders with his pace, power and trickery on the left of midfield. Had a terrific Champions League campaign. Named PFA Player of the Year.

PFA APPEARANCES: 1

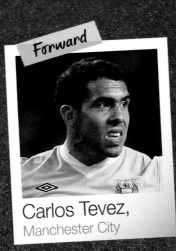

Forward

Carlos Tevez,
Manchester City

Missed out the previous campaign despite hitting 23 goals during his debut season at City. The Argentine couldn't be overlooked again as he struck 20 times in 31 league games, helping City to third. Tevez shared the league's Golden Boot Award. Assisted six, meaning he contributed to nearly half of the club's 60 league goals.

PFA APPEARANCES: 1

Forward

Dimitar Berbatov,
Manchester United

Scored his highest Premier League goals total in a season – 20 – to share the Golden Boot with Tevez. Had previously found life difficult at Old Trafford but put that to bed in a season of classy performances and goals. Scored hat-tricks against Liverpool and Birmingham and five against Blackburn. The Bulgarian fired United to a 19th title.

PFA APPEARANCES: 2

PFA TEAM OF THE YEAR 2011-2012

Goalkeeper

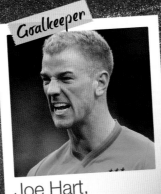

Joe Hart,
Manchester City

Helped City claim their first top-flight title for 44 years with 14 clean sheets. The ever-present conceded just 29 goals – the least in the division – and produced a series of top-class saves. His performances helped establish him as not only England's No.1 but also one of the best keepers in the world.

PFA APPEARANCES: 2

Defender

Kyle Walker,
Tottenham Hotspur

The right back produced many impressive performances during his breakthrough year at Tottenham. Played 37 matches and scored the winner against North London rivals Arsenal as Spurs finished fourth. Walker's form earned him a first England cap.

PFA APPEARANCES: 1

Defender

Fabricio Coloccini,
Newcastle United

The Magpies' captain led by example as Newcastle finished fifth – matching their final position of the 2003-04 season. Made an unimpressive start to his United career but flourished as the Toon cruised to the Championship title in 2010. Showed class both in and out of possession in all his 35 league appearances.

PFA APPEARANCES: 1

Defender

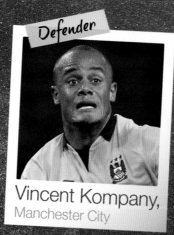

Vincent Kompany,
Manchester City

The Belgian was immense for boss Roberto Mancini. The City captain's perfect challenges, positioning and organisation played a major role in ensuring the title went to the blue half of Manchester. Formed an outstanding partnership with Joleon Lescott which saw his side keep 14 clean sheets. His winning header against rivals United at the end of the season was just one pivotal moment. Premier League Player of the Season.

PFA APPEARANCES: 2

Defender

Leighton Baines,
Everton

Ousted Ashley Cole from the Team of the Year and has since pushed the Chelsea man for his England place. Troubled many right backs with his penetrating runs down the flank. His wand of a left foot created two and scored four league goals. Part of a Toffees back four that held the joint third-best defensive record, having conceded 40 times.

PFA APPEARANCES: 1

David Silva,
Manchester City

The most creative player in the division with 17 assists. Scored six goals, including one in the 6-1 demolition of rivals United at Old Trafford. Used his trickery to consistently breeze by defenders and made the toughest passes look simple.

PFA APPEARANCES: 1

Yaya Toure,
Manchester City

The Ivory Coast star was unplayable at times in City's title-winning team. Despite missing a month due to African Nations Cup duty, the powerful midfielder was a big reason why the title went to Eastlands. Created eight and scored six – two in the penultimate fixture at Newcastle – in 32 league games.

PFA APPEARANCES: 1

Scott Parker,
Tottenham Hotspur

Had another impressive season after his move across London from West Ham. The midfielder's tough tackles and combative style complimented the flair of Luka Modric in the middle of the park. Also established himself in the England side.

PFA APPEARANCES: 1

Gareth Bale,
Tottenham Hotspur

Wing wizard Bale was at his glittering best throughout the season. Contributed to 20 of Spurs' goals – nine goals, 11 assists – and gave many a full-back a torrid time. The Welshman's form attracted Manchester United, Barcelona and Real Madrid.

PFA APPEARANCES: 3

Robin van Persie,
Arsenal

The Dutchman became the sixth player to hit 30 Premier League goals in a season as he helped Arsenal secure third. RVP scored with his left foot, right foot, headers, close and long range and assisted ten of the Gunners' goals. Won the Golden Boot for the first time in his eight-year Premier League career.

PFA APPEARANCES: 1

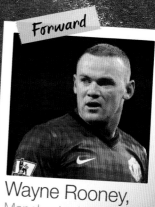

Wayne Rooney,
Manchester United

Had a terrific season once again and scored 27 league goals as United narrowly missed out to City on goal difference. Provided five assists for his team-mates. Reached the 150-goal mark for United in just over 350 games.

PFA APPEARANCES: 3

PFA TEAM OF THE YEAR 2012-2013

David De Gea,
Manchester United

After a difficult first season at Old Trafford, the Spaniard bounced back in terrific fashion. Kept 11 clean sheets in 34 Premier League games, as United regained the title. Made a number of world-class saves and was more confident, commanding and dominant between the sticks.

PFA APPEARANCES: 1

Pablo Zabaleta,
Manchester City

A consistent performer for City over the past few years, the Argentina international took his game to a new level. Was the club's star man in what was a disappointing and trophyless campaign. Played 30 league games in a defence that conceded just 34 times – the least in the division.

PFA APPEARANCES: 1

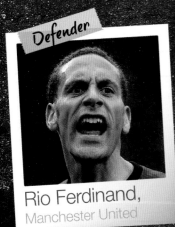

Rio Ferdinand,
Manchester United

After coming in for some criticism in recent seasons, Ferdinand proved why he is still one of the best defenders around, despite nearing the age of 35. Showed shrewd movement and positioning in his 28 league matches. Scored the winner, his first goal in five years, in the final home game of the season, against Swansea City.

PFA APPEARANCES: 6

Jan Vertonghen,
Tottenham Hotspur

The Belgian was monumental in his debut season in England. The £10m signing from Ajax made many vital challenges and set up numerous attacks with some pinpoint passing. His six Premier League goals, including a brace at Liverpool and a goal in the win at Manchester United, highlighted his value in both boxes.

PFA APPEARANCES: 1

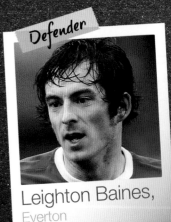

Leighton Baines,
Everton

The Everton ace again upped his challenge to become England's first-choice left back with another productive season. Defensively sound and a threat going forward, the 28-year-old was an ever-present in a side that finished sixth. Assisted seven goals and scored five, including a winning brace against West Brom.

PFA APPEARANCES: 2

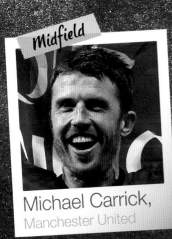

Midfield

Michael Carrick,
Manchester United

The cultured midfielder was the unsung hero in United's title-winning side. He claimed four assists and scored once in 36 starts for the Red Devils. But his calmness and accuracy on the ball started numerous attacking moves. The 31-year-old's form also saw him earn an England recall.

PFA APPEARANCES: 1

Midfield

Juan Mata,
Chelsea

The Spaniard carried on his fantastic form from his debut campaign at Stamford Bridge, creating 12 goals – the most in the Premier League. The playmaker would often conjure up a piece of magic for the Blues, who finished third and won the Europa League. The 25-year-old notched 19 goals in all competitions, including a crucial winner at Man United.

PFA APPEARANCES: 1

Midfield

Gareth Bale,
Tottenham Hotspur

The Welsh wizard was outstanding. Won the PFA Player and Young Player of the Year awards – just the third player to win both at the same time. Hit 31 goals – 21 in the league – as Spurs just missed the top-four. Scored numerous world-class goals from free-kicks and open play as he dazzled with pace, power and dribbling ability.

PFA APPEARANCES: 3

Midfield

Eden Hazard,
Chelsea

The Belgium star arrived in England for a whopping £32m, but the Blues were quickly rewarded with some dazzling displays. The 22-year-old scored nine times in 34 league games, including one in the 8-0 thrashing of Aston Villa. Created 11 goals for his team-mates.

PFA APPEARANCES: 1

Forward

Robin van Persie,
Manchester United

The difference in the title race! The Dutchman topped the scoring charts once again following his £24m move from Arsenal. Scored 26 times in the league, including vital strikes against Chelsea, Arsenal, Man City, and a title-clinching hat-trick at home to Aston Villa. Bailed the Red Devils out on a number of occasions and was unstoppable at times.

PFA APPEARANCES: 2

Forward

Luis Suarez,
Liverpool

Enjoyed a wonderful season as he put to bed his finishing problems of the previous year by scoring 31 times in 46 games. The Uruguay star was the second-highest scorer in the Premier League with 23 goals, and assisted seven. Missed the final four games of the season after he was handed a ten-match ban for biting Chelsea's Branislav Ivanovic!

PFA APPEARANCES: 1

PREMIER LEAGUE
PFA ALL TIME APPEARANCE
MAKERS XI

Goalkeeper

Nigel Martyn
CLUBS WHEN NOMINATED
Leeds United
PFA APPEARANCES 3
(1998, 1999, 2000)
**PREMIER LEAGUE
SEASONS** 11
**PREMIER LEAGUE
APPEARANCES** 371
**PREMIER LEAGUE CLEAN
SHEETS** 138
*Edwin van der Sar has also
appeared three times but kept
less clean sheets than Martyn.
* All details correct to end of
season 2012-13.*

Defender

Ashley Cole
CLUBS WHEN NOMINATED
Arsenal, Chelsea
PFA APPEARANCES 4
(2003, 2004, 2005, 2011)
PREMIER LEAGUE SEASONS 14
**PREMIER LEAGUE
APPEARANCES** 367
PREMIER LEAGUE GOALS 15

Defender

Nemanja Vidic
CLUBS WHEN NOMINATED
Manchester United
PFA APPEARANCES 4
(2007, 2008, 2009, 2011)
PREMIER LEAGUE SEASONS 8
**PREMIER LEAGUE
APPEARANCES** 186
PREMIER LEAGUE GOALS 15

Defender

Rio Ferdinand
CLUBS WHEN NOMINATED
Leeds United, Manchester United
PFA APPEARANCES 6
(2002, 2005, 2007, 2008, 2009, 2013)
PREMIER LEAGUE SEASONS 18
**PREMIER LEAGUE
APPEARANCES** 478
PREMIER LEAGUE GOALS 11

Defender

Gary Neville
CLUBS WHEN NOMINATED
Manchester United
PFA APPEARANCES 6
(1996, 1997, 1998, 1999, 2005, 2007)
PREMIER LEAGUE SEASONS 17
**PREMIER LEAGUE
APPEARANCES** 397
PREMIER LEAGUE GOALS 5

Roy Keane

CLUBS WHEN NOMINATED
Nottingham Forest, Manchester United
PFA APPEARANCES 5
(1993, 1997, 2000, 2001, 2002)
PREMIER LEAGUE SEASONS 14
**PREMIER LEAGUE
APPEARANCES** 366
PREMIER LEAGUE GOALS 39

Midfield

Patrick Vieira

CLUBS WHEN NOMINATED
Arsenal
PFA APPEARANCES 6
(1999, 2000, 2001, 2002, 2003, 2004)
PREMIER LEAGUE SEASONS 11
**PREMIER LEAGUE
APPEARANCES** 307
PREMIER LEAGUE GOALS 33

Forward

Alan Shearer

CLUBS WHEN NOMINATED
Blackburn Rovers, Newcastle United
PFA APPEARANCES 6
(1993, 1994, 1995, 1996, 1997, 2003)
PREMIER LEAGUE SEASONS 14
**PREMIER LEAGUE
APPEARANCES** 441
PREMIER LEAGUE GOALS 260

Midfield

Steven Gerrard

CLUBS WHEN NOMINATED
Liverpool
PFA APPEARANCES 7
(2001, 2004, 2005, 2006, 2007,
2008, 2009)
PREMIER LEAGUE SEASONS 21
**PREMIER LEAGUE
APPEARANCES** 439
PREMIER LEAGUE GOALS 98

Midfield

Ryan Giggs

CLUBS WHEN NOMINATED
Manchester United
PFA APPEARANCES 6
(1993, 1998, 2001, 2002,
2007, 2009)
PREMIER LEAGUE SEASONS 14
**PREMIER LEAGUE
APPEARANCES** 620
PREMIER LEAGUE GOALS 109

Forward

Thierry Henry

CLUBS WHEN NOMINATED
Arsenal
PFA APPEARANCES 6
(2001, 2002, 2003, 2004, 2005, 2006)
PREMIER LEAGUE SEASONS 9
**PREMIER LEAGUE
APPEARANCES** 258
PREMIER LEAGUE GOALS 176

FRENCH
PLAYER OF THE YEAR

Former Arsenal striker Thierry Henry has been French Player of the year a staggering five times, including four consecutive seasons.

Up to 1995 only players turning out in their home country were eligible to win the award. Since 2001 only former winners get a say in who should collect the trophy.

1976

1990

ALL THE WINNERS...

1959	Jules Sbroglia, Angers	**1990**	Laurent Blanc, Montpellier
1960	Raymond Kopa, Stade Reims	**1991**	Jean-Pierre Papin, Marseille
1961	Mahi Khennane, Rennes	**1992**	Alain Roche, Auxerre
1962	Andre Lerond, Stade Francais	**1993**	David Ginola, Paris Saint-Germain
1963	Yvon Douis, Monaco	**1994**	Bernard Lama, Paris Saint-Germain
1964	Marcel Artelesa, Monaco	**1995**	Vincent Guerin, Paris Saint-Germain
1965	Phillipe Gondet, Nantes	**1996**	Didier Deschamps, Juventus
1966	Phillipe Gondet, Nantes	**1997**	Lilian Thuram, Parma
1967	Bernard Bosquier, Saint-Etienne	**1998**	Zinedine Zidane, Juventus
1968	Bernard Bosquier, Saint-Etienne	**1999**	Sylvain Wiltord, Bordeaux
1969	Herve Revelli, Saint-Etienne	**2000**	Thierry Henry, Arsenal
1970	Georges, Carnus, Saint-Etienne	**2001**	Patrick Vieira, Arsenal
1971	Georges, Carnus, Saint-Etienne	**2002**	Zinedine Zidane, Real Madrid
1972	Marius Tresor, Ajaccio	**2003**	Thierry Henry, Arsenal
1973	Georges Bereta, Saint-Etienne	**2004**	Thierry Henry, Arsenal
1974	Georges Bereta, Saint-Etienne	**2005**	Thierry Henry, Arsenal
1975	Jean-Marc Guillou, Angers	**2006**	Thierry Henry, Arsenal
1976	Michel Platini, Nancy	**2007**	Franck Ribery, Marseille
1977	Michel Platini, Nancy	**2008**	Franck Ribery, Bayern Munich
1978	Jean Petit, Monaco	**2009**	Yoann Gourcuff, Bordeaux
1979	Maxime Bossis, Nantes	**2010**	Samir Nasri, Arsenal
1980	Jean-Francois Larios, Saint-Etienne	**2011**	Karim Benzema, Real Madrid
1981	Maxime Bossis, Nantes	**2012**	Karim Benzema, Real Madrid
1982	Alain Giresse, Bordeaux		
1983	Alain Giresse, Bordeaux		
1984	Jean Tigana, Bordeaux		
1985	Luis Fernandez, Paris Saint-Germain		
1986	Manuel Amoros, Monaco		
1987	Alain Giresse, Bordeaux		
1988	Stephane Paille, Sochaux		
1989	Jean-Pierre Papin, Marseille		

2012

GERMAN
FOOTBALLER OF THE YEAR

Football journalists in the country vote for the German Footballer of the Year. All German footballers are eligible, whether playing at home or abroad. Foreign players in German football can also win.

No surprise that players of Bayern Munich dominate the awards – but the club's France winger, Franck Ribery, won the title at the same time as he became his own country's Player of the Year.

ALL THE WINNERS...

1960	Uwe Seeler, Hamburg	**1991**	Stefan Kuntz, Kaiserslautern
1961	Max Morlock, Nuremburg	**1992**	Thomas Habler, Roma
1962	Karl-Heinz Schnellinger, Cologne	**1993**	Andreas, Kopke, Nuremburg
1963	Hans Schafer, Cologne	**1994**	Jurgen Klinsman, Monaco
1964	Uwe Seeler, Hamburg	**1995**	Matthias Sammer, Borussia Dortmund
1965	Hans Tilkowski, Borussia Dortmund	**1996**	Matthias Sammer, Borussia Dortmund
1966	Franz Beckenbauer, Bayern Munich	**1997**	Jurgen Kohler, Borussia Dortmund
1967	Gerd Muller, Bayern Munich	**1998**	Oliver Bierhoff, Udinese
1968	Franz Beckenbauer, Bayern Munich	**1999**	Lothar Matthaus, Bayern Munich
1969	Gerd Muller, Bayern Munich	**2000**	Oliver Kahn, Bayern Munich
1970	Uwe Seeler, Hamburg	**2001**	Oliver Kahn, Bayern Munich
1971	Berti Vogts, Borussia Monchengladbach	**2002**	Michael Ballack, Bayer Leverkusen
1972	Gunter Netzer, Borussia Monchengladbach	**2003**	Michael Ballack, Bayern Munich
1973	Gunter Netzer, Borussia Monchengladbach	**2004**	Ailton, Werder Bremen
1974	Franz Beckenbauer, Bayern Munich	**2005**	Michael Ballack, Bayern Munich
1975	Sepp Maier, Bayern Munich	**2006**	Miroslav Klose, Werder Bremen
1976	Franz Beckenbauer, Bayern Munich	**2007**	Mario Gomez, Stuttgart
1977	Sepp Maier, Bayern Munich	**2008**	Franck Ribery, Bayern Munich
1978	Sepp Maier, Bayern Munich	**2009**	Grafite, Wolfsburg
1979	Berti Vogts, Borussia Monchengladbach	**2010**	Arjen Robben, Bayern Munich
1980	Karl-Heinze Rummenigge, Bayern Munich	**2011**	Manuel Neuer, Schalke 04
1981	Paul Breitner, Bayner Munich	**2012**	Marco Reus, Borussia Monchengladbach
1982	Karlheinz Forster, Stuttgart		
1983	Rudi Voller, Werder Bremen		
1984	Harald Schumacher, Cologne		
1985	Hans-Peter Briegel, Verona		
1986	Harald Schumacher, Cologne		
1987	Uwe Rahn, Borussia Monchengladbach		
1988	Jurgen Klinsmann, Stuttgart		
1989	Thomas Habler, Cologne		
1990	Lothar Matthaus, Inter Milan		

SPAIN
FOOTBALLER OF THE YEAR

The Don Balon Award went to the best Spanish footballer each campaign until the end of season 2009-10. The awards were handed out by the Spanish magazine of the same name until it ceased publication in 2011.

Record-breaking striker Raul won the award five times, during his time at Real Madrid, including four consecutive seasons. The Liga de Futbol Profesional, which was established in 2008, now hands out official awards which include Best Player.

1998

2004

ALL THE WINNERS…

Don Balon

1976 Miguel Angel Gonzalez, Real Madrid
1977 Juanito, Burgos
1978 Migueli, Barcelona
1979 Quini, Sporting Gijon
1980 Rafael Gordillo, Betis
1981 Urruti, Espanyol
1982 Miguel Tendillo, Valencia
1983 Juan Senor, Real Zaragoza
1984 Manuel Cervantes, Real Murcia
1985 Migueli, Barcelona
1986 Michel, Real Madrid
1987 Andoni Zubizareta, Barcelona
1988 Juan Antonio Larranaga, Real Sociedad
1989 Fernando Gomez, Valencia
1990 Rafael Martin Vazquez, Real Madrid
1991 Jon Andoni Goikoetxea, Barcelona
1992 Agustin Elduayen, Burgos
1993 Fran Gonzalez, Deportivo de La Coruna
1994 Julen Guerrero, Athletic Bilbao
1995 Jose Emilio Amavisca, Real Madrid
1996 Jose Luis Perez Caminero, Atletico Madrid

1997 Raul Gonzalez, Real Madrid
1998 Alfonso Perez, Betis
1999 Raul Gonzalez, Real Madrid
2000 Raul Gonzalez, Real Madrid
2001 Raul Gonzalez, Real Madrid
2002 Raul Gonzalez, Real Madrid
2003 Xabi Alonso, Real Sociedad
2004 Vicente Rodriguez, Valencia
2005 Xavi Hernandez, Barcelona
2006 David Villa, Valencia
2007 Santi Cazorla, Recreativo de Huelva
2008 Marcos Senna, Villarreal
2009 Andres Iniesta, Barcelona
2010 Borja Valero, RCD Mallorca

LFP Awards

2009 Lionel Messi, Barcelona
2010 Lionel Messi, Barcelona
2011 Lionel Messi, Barcelona
2012 Lionel Messi, Barcelona

2009

2012

ITALY
FOOTBALLER OF THE YEAR

Footballers in Italy used to compete for three major awards – the Italian Footballer of the Year, Serie A Foreign Footballer of the Year and Serie A Footballer of the Year.

But the format of the awards was changed in 2011 and replaced by a Grand Gala of football to produce just one winner, the best player in Serie A over the previous season. Long-serving Roma forward Franceso Totti and Sweden striker Zlatan Ibrahimovic are two of the best performers in these awards.

Del Piero 2008

Totti 2001

Batistuta 1999

ALL THE WINNERS...

Italian Footballer of the Year

1997 Roberto Mancini, Sampdoria
1998 Alessandro Del Piero, Juventus
1999 Christian Vieri, Lazio
2000 Francesco Totti, Roma
2001 Francesco Totti, Roma
2002 Christian Vieri, Inter Milan
2003 Francesco Totti, Roma
2004 Francesco Totti, Roma
2005 Alberto Gilardino, Parma
2006 Fabio Cannavaro, Juventus
2007 Francesco Totti, Roma
2008 Alessandro Del Piero, Juventus
2009 Daniele De Rossi, Roma
2010 Antonio Di Natale, Udinese

Serie A Foreign Footballer of the Year

1997 Zinedine Zidane, Juventus
1998 Ronaldo, Inter Milan
1999 Gabriel Batistuta, Fiorentina
2000 Andriy Shevchenko, AC Milan
2001 Zinedine Zidane, Juventus
2002 David Trezeguet, Juventus
2003 Pavel Nedved, Juventus
2004 Kaka, AC Milan
2005 Zlatan Ibrahimovic, Juventus
2006 Kaka, AC Milan
         David Suazo, Cagliari
2007 Kaka, AC Milan
2008 Zlatan Ibrahimovic, Inter Milan

2009 Zlatan Ibrahimovic, Inter Milan
2010 Diego Milito, Inter Milan

Serie A Footballer of the Year

1997 Roberto Mancini, Sampdoria
1998 Ronaldo, Inter Milan
1999 Christian Vieri, Lazio
2000 Francesco Totti, Roma
2001 Zinedine Zidane, Juventus
2002 David Trezeguet, Juventus
2003 Pavel Nedved, Juventus
         Franceso Totti, Roma
2004 Kaka, AC Milan
2005 Alberto Gilardino, Parma
2006 Fabio Cannavaro, Juventus
2007 Kaka, AC Milan
2008 Zlatan Ibramhimovic, Inter Milan
2009 Zlatan Ibramhimovic, Inter Milan
2010 Diego Milito, Inter Milan
2011 Zlatan Ibrahimovic, AC Milan
2012 Andrea Pirlo, Juventus

Kaka 2007

DUTCH
FOOTBALLER OF THE YEAR

Players in Holland's top two leagues vote for the Dutch Footballer of the Year.

The Golden Shoe, which had been awarded since 1982 by the newspaper De Telegraaf and magazine Voetbal International, merged with the main title in 2006. The first non-Dutchman to win either award was Brazil striker Romario in 1989, just a year after arriving at PSV.

2002

1984

2005

ALL THE WINNERS...

Footballer of the Year

1984	Ruud Gullit, Feyenoord
1985	Marco Van Basten, Ajax
1986	Ruud Gullit, PSV Eindhoven
1987	Ronald Koeman, PSV Eindhoven
1988	Ronald Koeman, PSV Eindhoven
1989	Romario, PSV Eindhoven
1990	Jan Wouters, Ajax
1991	Dennis Bergkamp, Ajax
1992	Dennis Bergkamp, Ajax
1993	Jari Litmanen, Ajax
1994	Ronald de Boer, Ajax
1995	Luc Nilis, PSV Eindhoven
1996	Ronald de Boer, Ajax
1997	Jaap Stam, PSV Eindhoven
1999	Ruud van Nistelrooy, PSV Eindhoven
2000	Ruud van Nistelrooy, PSV Eindhoven
2001	Mark van Bommel, PSV Eindhoven
2002	Pierre van Hooijdonk, Feyenoord
2003	Mateja Kezman, PSV Eindhoven
2004	Maxwell, Ajax
2005	Mark van Bommel, PSV Eindhoven

*Award changed from annual to end of season in 1997, hence no 1998 award.

Golden Shoe

1982	Martin Haar, Haarlem
1983	Piet Schrijvers, Ajax
1984	Johan Cruyff, Feyenoord
1985	Frank Rijkaard, Ajax
1986	Ruud Gullit, PSV Eindhoven
1987	Frank Rijkaard, Ajax
1988	Gerald Vanenburg, PSV Eindhoven

1989	Gerald Vanenburg, PSV Eindhoven
1990	Edward Sturing, Vitesse
1991	Hennie Meijer, Groningen
1992	John Metgod, Feyenoord
1993	Marc Overmars, Ajax
1994	Ed de Goey, Feyenoord
1995	Danny Blind, Ajax
1996	Danny Blind, Ajax
1997	Jaap Stam, PSV Eindhoven
1998	Edwin van der Sar, Ajax
1999	Michael Mols, Utrecht
2000	Jerzy Dudek, Feyenoord
2001	Johann Vogel, PSV Eindhoven
2002	Cristian Chivu, Ajax
2005	Mark van Bommel, PSV Eindhoven

Joint award

2006	Dirk Kuyt, Feyenoord
2007	Afonso Alves, Heerenveen
2008	John Heitinga, Ajax
2009	Mounir El Hamadaoui, Az Alkmaar
2010	Luis Suarez, Ajax
2011	Theo Janssen, Twente
2012	Jan Vertonghen, Ajax
2013	Wilfried Boney, Vitesse

2013

GOLDEN GUYS

The hot-shot strikers who have won the Premier League's Golden Boot for being the competition's top scorers

1992-93
GOALS 22
Teddy Sheringham
Tottenham Hotspur

1993-94
GOALS 34
Andy Cole
Newcastle United

1994-95
GOALS 34
Alan Shearer
Blackburn Rovers

1995-96
GOALS 34
Alan Shearer
Blackburn Rovers

1996-97
GOALS 25
Alan Shearer
Newcastle United

1997-98
GOALS 18
Chris Sutton
Blackburn Rovers

Michael Owen
Liverpool

Dion Dublin,
Coventry City

1998-99
GOALS 18
Dwight Yorke
Manchester United

Michael Owen
Liverpool

Jimmy Floyd-Hasselbaink
Leeds United

1999-00
GOALS 30
Kevin Phillips
Sunderland

2008-09
GOALS
19
Nicolas Anelka
Chelsea

2009-10
GOALS
29
Didier Drogba
Chelsea

2000-01
GOALS
23
Jimmy Floyd Hasselbaink
Chelsea

2004-05
GOALS
25
Thierry Henry
Arsenal

2010-11
GOALS
20
Carlos Tevez
Manchester City

Dimitar Berbatov
Manchester United

2001-02
GOALS
24
Thierry Henry
Arsenal

2005-06
GOALS
27
Thierry Henry
Arsenal

2002-03
GOALS
25
Ruud Van Nistelrooy
Manchester United

2006-07
GOALS
20
Didier Drogba
Chelsea

2011-12
GOALS
30
Robin Van Persie
Arsenal

2003-04
GOALS
30
Thierry Henry
Arsenal

2007-08
GOALS
31
Cristiano Ronaldo
Manchester United

2012-13
GOALS
26
Robin Van Persie
Manchester United

SAFE HANDS!

The Premier League Golden Glove award goes to the goalkeeper who has kept the most clean sheets during a season. It has run from season 2004-05.

2004-05
Petr Cech,
Chelsea

CLEAN SHEETS
21

2005-06
Pepe Reina,
Liverpool

CLEAN SHEETS
20

2006-07
Pepe Reina,
Liverpool

CLEAN SHEETS
19

2007-08
Pepe Reina,
Liverpool

CLEAN SHEETS
18

2008-09
Edwin van der Sar,
Manchester United

CLEAN SHEETS
21

2009-10
Petr Cech,
Chelsea

CLEAN SHEETS
17

2010-11
Joe Hart,
Manchester City

CLEAN SHEETS
18

2011-12
Joe Hart,
Manchester City

CLEAN SHEETS
17

2012-13
Joe Hart,
Manchester City

CLEAN SHEETS
18

*Reina also had 17 clean sheets in 2009-10, but Cech had a better ratio compared to games played.

WORLD
CUP
STARS

It's the biggest football tournament on the planet so no surprise that there are plenty of awards to be won besides the World Cup itself! The coveted prize after the trophy that goes to the top team is the Golden Ball for the best player at the FIFA-organised event. There are also Silver and Bronze Balls for the second and third best players at each tournament.

1938

1958

1966

1970

YEAR	GOLD	SILVER	BRONZE
1930	Jose Nasazzi (Uruguay)	Guillermo Stabile (Argentina)	Jose Andrade (Uruguay)
1934	Giuseppe Meazza (Italy)	Matthias Sindelar (Austria)	Oldrich Nejedly (Czechoslovakia)
1938	Leonidas (Brazil)	Silvio Piola (Italy)	Gyorgy Sarosi (Hungary)
1950	Zizinho (Brazil)	Juan Schiaffino (Uruguay)	Ademire (Brazil)
1954	Ferenc Puskas (Hungary)	Sandor Kocsis (Hungary)	Fritz Walter (West Germany)
1958	Didi (Brazil)	Pele (Brazil)	Just Fontaine (France)
1962	Garrincha (Brazil)	Josef Masopust (Czech)	Leonel Sanchez (Chile)
1966	Bobby Charlton (England)	Bobby Moore (England)	Eusebio (Portugal)
1970	Pele (Brazil)	Gerson (Brazil)	Gerd Muller (West Germany)
1974	Johan Cruyff (Holland)	Franz Beckenbauer (W Germ)	Kazimierz Deyna (Poland)
1978	Mario Kempes (Argentina)	Paolo Rossi (Italy)	Dirceu (Brazil)
1982	Paolo Rossi (Italy)	Falcao (Brazil)	Karl-Heinz Rummenigge (Germ)
1986	Diego Maradona (Arg)	Harald Schumacher (Germ)	Preben Elkjaer Larsen (Denmark)
1990	Salvatore Schillaci (Italy)	Lothar Mattaus (Germany)	Diego Maradona (Argentina)
1994	Romario (Brazil)	Roberto Baggio (Italy)	Hristo Stoichkov (Bulgaria)
1998	Ronaldo (Brazil)	Davor Suker (Croatia)	Lilian Thuram (France)
2002	Oliver Kahn (Germany)	Ronaldo (Brazil)	Hong Myung-Bo (South Korea)
2006	Zinedine Zidane (France)	Fabio Cannavaro (Italy)	Andrea Pirlo (Italy)
2010	Diego Forlan (Uruguay)	Wesley Sneijder (Holland)	David Villa (Spain)

1982

1994

2002

2010

Euro Stars

The European Championships are played every four years – sandwiched between World Cup finals. The Player of the Tournament award has only been handed out since 1996 and to a member of the winning team. UEFA have always kept records of the top scorers.

Player of the Tournament

1996

Matthias Sammer
Germany

2000

Zinedine Zidane
France

2004

Theodoros Zagorakis
Greece

2008

Xavi
Spain

2012

Andres Iniesta
Spain

Top Scorers

1960
Francois Heutte (France), **Valentin Ivanov,** (Soviet Union), **Viktor Ponedelnik** (Soviet Union), **Milan Galic** (SFR Yugoslavia) **Drazan Jerkovic** (SFR Yugoslavia) 2

1964
Jesus Maria Pereda (Spain), **Ferenc Bene** (Hungary), **Dezso Novak** (Hungary) 2

1968
Dragan Dzajic (SFR Yugoslavia) 2

1972
Gerd Muller (West Germany) 4

1976
Dieter Muller (West Germany) 4

1980
Klaus Allofs (West Germany) 3

1984
Michel Platini (France) 9

1988
Marco Van Basten (Holland) 5

1992
Henrik Larsen (Denmark), **Karl-Heinz Riedle** (Germany), **Dennis Bergkamp** (Holland), **Tomas Brolin** (Sweden) 3

1996
Alan Shearer (England) 5

1996

2000
Patrick Kluivert (Holland), **Savo Milosevic** (FR Yugoslavia) 5

2004
Milan Baros (Czech Republic) 5

2008
David Villa (Spain) 4

2012
Mario Mandzukic (Croatia), **Mario Gomez** (Germany), **Mario Balotelli** (Italy), **Cristiano Ronaldo** (Portugal), **Alan Dzagoev** (Russia), **Fernando Torres** (Spain) 3

INTERNATIONAL SUPERSTARS

The players who have made the most appearances for some of Europe's biggest sides.

ENGLAND

PETER SHILTON

APPEARANCES: 125 **POSITION:** Keeper
INTERNATIONAL DEBUT: 1970 **LAST GAME:** 1990
CLUBS: Leicester City, Stoke City, Nottingham Forest, Southampton, Derby County

SCOTLAND

KENNY DALGLISH

APPEARANCES: 102
POSITION: Forward
INTERNATIONAL DEBUT: 1971
LAST GAME: 1986 **CLUBS:** Celtic, Liverpool

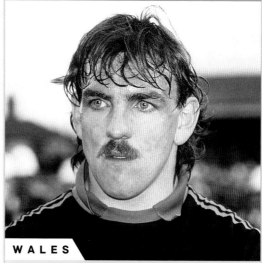

WALES

NEVILLE SOUTHALL

APPEARANCES: 92
POSITION: Keeper
INTERNATIONAL DEBUT: 1982
LAST GAME: 1997 **CLUBS:** Everton

REPUBLIC OF IRELAND

ROBBIE KEANE

APPEARANCES: 127
POSITION: Striker **INTERNATIONAL DEBUT:** 1998
LAST GAME: Still playing **CLUBS:** Wolves, Coventry, Inter Milan, Leeds United, Tottenham, Liverpool, Celtic (loan), West Ham (loan), LA Galaxy, Aston Villa (loan)

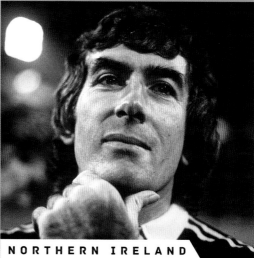

NORTHERN IRELAND

PAT JENNINGS

APPEARANCES: 119
POSITION: Keeper **INTERNATIONAL DEBUT:** 1964
LAST GAME: 1986
CLUBS: Watford, Tottenham, Arsenal

IKER CASILLAS

APPEARANCES: 146 **POSITION:** Keeper
INTERNATIONAL DEBUT: 2000
LAST GAME: Still playing
CLUBS: Real Madrid

ITALY

FABIO CANNAVARO

APPEARANCES: 136 **POSITION:** Defender
INTERNATIONAL DEBUT: 1997
LAST GAME: 2010
CLUBS: Parma, Inter Milan, Juventus, Real Madrid

GERMANY

LOTHAR MATTHAUS

APPEARANCES: 150 **POSITION:** Midfielder
INTERNATIONAL DEBUT: 1980 **LAST GAME:** 2000
CLUBS: Borussia Monchengladbach, Bayern Munich, Inter Milan

HOLLAND

EDWIN VAN DER SAR

APPEARANCES: 130 **POSITION:** Keeper
INTERNATIONAL DEBUT: 1994
LAST GAME: 2008
CLUBS: Ajax, Juventus, Fulham, Manchester United

FRANCE

LILIAN THURAM

APPEARANCES: 142 **POSITION:** Defender
INTERNATIONAL DEBUT: 1994
LAST GAME: 2008
CLUBS: Monaco, Parma, Juventus, Barcelona

DENMARK

PETER SCHMEICHEL

APPEARANCES: 129 **POSITION:** Keeper
INTERNATIONAL DEBUT: 1987 **LAST GAME:** 2001
CLUBS: Brondby, Manchester United, Sporting Lisbon, Aston Villa, Manchester City

SWEDEN

THOMAS RAVELLI

APPEARANCES: 143 **POSITION:** Keeper
INTERNATIONAL DEBUT: 1981
LAST GAME: 1997
CLUBS: Oster, IFK Gothenburg

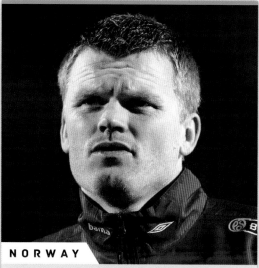

NORWAY

JOHN ARNE RIISE

APPEARANCES: 110 **POSITION:** Defender
INTERNATIONAL DEBUT: 2000
LAST GAME: 2012
CLUBS: Monaco, Liverpool, Roma, Fulham

STIPE PLETIKOSA

APPEARANCES: 103 **POSITION:** Keeper
INTERNATIONAL DEBUT: 1999
LAST GAME: Still playing **CLUBS:** Hajduk Split,
Shakhtar Donetsk, Spartak Moscow, Rostov

RUSSIA

VIKTOR ONOPKO

APPEARANCES: **POSITION:** Defender
INTERNATIONAL DEBUT: 1992 **LAST GAME:** 2004
CLUBS: Spartak Moscow, Real Oviedo, Ray Vallecano,
Alania Vladikavkaz, Saturn Moscow

CROATIA

DARIJO SRNA

APPEARANCES: 104 **POSITION:** Defender-midfielder
INTERNATIONAL DEBUT: 2002
LAST GAME: Still playing
CLUBS: Hajduk Split, Shakhtar Donetsk

LUIS FIGO

APPEARANCES: 127 **POSITION:** Midfielder
INTERNATIONAL DEBUT: 1991 **LAST GAME:** 2006
CLUBS: Sporting Lisbon, Barcelona,
Real Madrid, Inter Milan

GREECE

THEO ZAGORAKIS

APPEARANCES: 120 **POSITION:** Midfielder
INTERNATIONAL DEBUT: 1994
LAST GAME: 2007
CLUBS: PAOK, Leicester City, AEK Athens, Bologna

GREECE

GIORGIOS KARAGOUNIS

APPEARANCES: 125 **POSITION:** Midfielder
INTERNATIONAL DEBUT: 1999
LAST GAME: Still playing
CLUBS: Panathinaikos, Inter Milan, Benfica, Fulham

SWITZERLAND

HEINZ HERMANN

APPEARANCES: 118 **POSITION:** Midfielder
INTERNATIONAL DEBUT: 1978
LAST GAME: 1991
CLUBS: Grasshopper Zurich, Neuchatel Xamax, Servette

BELGIUM

JAN CEULEMANS

APPEARANCES: 96 **POSITION:** Midfielder
INTERNATIONAL DEBUT: 1977
LAST GAME: 1991
CLUBS: Lierse, Club Brugge

BOSNIA

ZVJEZDAN MISIMOVIC

APPEARANCES: 72 **POSITION:** Midfielder
INTERNATIONAL DEBUT: 2004 **LAST GAME:**
Still playing **CLUBS:** Bayern Munich, Bochum, Nuremburg, Wolfsburg, Galatasaray, Dynamo Moscow, Guizhou Renhe

CZECH REPUBLIC

KAREL POBORSKY

APPEARANCES: 118 **POSITION:** Winger
INTERNATIONAL DEBUT: 1994 **LAST GAME:** 2006
CLUBS: Viktoria Zizkov, Slavia Prague, Manchester United, Benfica, Lazio, Sparta Prague, Ceske Budejovice

* Only clubs listed where player played whilst an international

YOUR GUIDE TO THE BEST OF 2012-13

All of the English and Scottish League tables, top scorers, best managers, leading players, crowds – plus a special report on Manchester United's 20th top-flight title.

PREMIER LEAGUE FINAL TABLE 2012-13

With the title won and relegation settled it was the battle for Champions League spots that dominated the final day of the term

With the title and relegation issues sorted before the final day it was the race for the final two Champions League spots that hogged the headlines.

Manchester United and Manchester City had already booked their places at Europe's top table. Chelsea's 2-1 victory over Everton ensured they ended third.

Arsenal needed to win at Newcastle to grab fourth spot ahead of North London rivals Tottenham. The Gunners won 1-0, the same scoreline that Spurs managed at home to Sunderland.

Arsene Wenger's side qualifed for the Champions League for a sixteenth consecutive season.

Luis Suarez, Liverpool

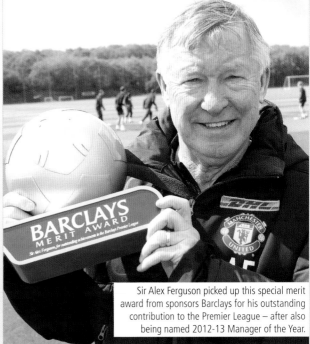
Sir Alex Ferguson picked up this special merit award from sponsors Barclays for his outstanding contribution to the Premier League – after also being named 2012-13 Manager of the Year.

TOP SCORERS

26	**Robin van Persie** (Man United)	
23	**Luis Suarez** (Liverpool)	
21	**Gareth Bale** (Tottenham)	
19	**Christian Benteke** (Aston Villa)	
18	**Michu** (Swansea)	
17	**Romelo Lukaku** (West Brom)	
15	**Demba Ba** (Chelsea*),	

Dimitar Berbatov (Fulham),
Rickie Lambert (Southampton)
and **Frank Lampard** (Chelsea)
* 13 for Newcastle United

Robin Van Persie, Manchester United

2013

POS	TEAM	P	W	D	L	F	A	GD	PTS
1	**Manchester United**	38	28	5	5	86	43	43	89
2	**Manchester City**	38	23	9	6	66	34	32	78
3	**Chelsea**	38	22	9	7	75	39	36	75
4	**Arsenal**	38	21	10	7	72	37	35	73
5	**Tottenham**	38	21	9	8	66	46	20	72
6	**Everton**	38	16	15	7	55	40	15	63
7	**Liverpool**	38	16	13	9	71	43	28	61
8	**West Brom**	38	14	7	17	53	57	-4	49
9	**Swansea City**	38	11	13	14	47	51	-4	46
10	**West Ham**	38	12	10	16	45	53	-8	46
11	**Norwich City**	38	10	14	14	41	58	-17	44
12	**Fulham**	38	11	10	17	50	60	-10	43
13	**Stoke City**	38	9	15	14	34	45	-11	42
14	**Southampton**	38	9	14	15	49	60	-11	41
15	**Aston Villa**	38	10	11	17	47	69	-22	41
16	**Newcastle United**	38	11	8	19	45	68	-23	41
17	**Sunderland**	38	9	12	17	41	54	-13	39
18	**Wigan Athletic**	38	9	9	20	47	73	-26	36
19	**Reading**	38	6	10	22	43	73	-30	28
20	**Queens Park Rangers**	38	4	13	21	30	60	-30	25

MANAGERS OF THE MONTH

September: David Moyes (Everton)
October: Sir Alex Ferguson (Manchester United)
November: Steve Clarke (West Brom)
December: Andre Villas-Boas (Tottenham)
January: Brian McDermott (Reading)
February: Andre Villas-Boas (Tottenham)
March: David Moyes (Everton)
April: Rafa Benitez (Chelsea)
Manager of the Year: Sir Alex Ferguson

PFA TEAM OF THE YEAR

David de Gea (Manchester United), **Pablo Zabaleta** (Manchester City), **Jan Vertonghen** (Tottenham), **Rio Ferdinand** (Manchester United), **Leighton Baines** (Everton), **Michael Carrick** (Manchester United), **Juan Mata** (Chelsea), **Gareth Bale** (Tottenham Hotspur), **Eden Hazard** (Chelsea), **Luis Suarez** (Liverpool), **Robin van Persie** (Manchester United).

CHAMPIONSHIP
FINAL TABLE 2012-13

With Cardiff City's promotion already confirmed before the final day it was a straight fight between Hull City and Watford for the final automatic place in the Premier League.

Steve Bruce's Tigers drew 2-2 at home to the champions and then had to watch as Watford – minus their two regular keepers – played out the remaining minutes of their home game with Leeds.

A win would have given the Hornets the automatic place on goal difference, but they were beaten 2-1, the winner coming in the final seconds of the game.

The play-off semi-finals saw Watford beat Leicester and Crystal Palace despatch Brighton.

Palace defeated Watford 1-0 in the final thanks to an extra-time penalty by veteran striker Kevin Phillips, a 67th minute substitute.

Jordan Rhodes, Blackburn

TOP SCORERS

- 30 **Glenn Murray** (Crystal Palace)
- 28 **Jordan Rhodes** (Blackburn)
- 24 **Charlie Austin** (Burnley)
- 20 **Chris Wood** (Leicester) and **Matej Vydrda** (Watford)
- 19 **Troy Deeney** (Watford)
- 18 **Tom Ince** (Blackpool)
- 16 **Luciano Becchio** (Leeds)
- 14 **James Vaughan** (Huddersfield), **David Nugent** (Leicester) and **Sylvan Ebanks-Blake** (Wolves)

Glenn Murray, Crystal Palace

POS	TEAM	P	W	D	L	F	A	GD	PTS
1	Cardiff City	46	25	12	9	72	45	27	87
2	Hull City	46	24	7	15	61	52	9	79
3	Watford	46	23	8	15	85	58	27	77
4	Brighton	46	19	18	9	69	43	26	75
5	Crystal Palace	46	19	15	12	73	62	11	72
6	Leicester City	46	19	11	16	71	48	23	68
7	Bolton	46	18	14	14	69	61	8	68
8	Nottingham Forest	46	17	16	13	63	59	4	67
9	Charlton	46	17	14	15	65	59	6	65
10	Derby County	46	16	13	17	65	62	3	61
11	Burnley	46	16	13	17	62	60	2	61
12	Birmingham	46	15	16	15	63	69	-6	6
13	Leeds United	46	17	10	19	57	66	-9	61
14	Ipswich Town	46	16	12	18	48	61	-13	60
15	Blackpool	46	14	17	15	62	63	-1	59
16	Middlesbrough	46	18	5	23	61	70	-9	59
17	Blackburn	46	14	16	16	55	62	-7	58
18	Sheffield Wednesday	46	16	10	20	53	61	-8	58
19	Huddersfield	46	15	13	18	53	73	-20	58
20	Millwall	46	15	11	20	51	62	-11	56
21	Barnsley	46	14	13	19	56	70	-14	55
22	Peterborough	46	15	9	22	66	75	-9	54
23	Wolves	46	14	9	23	55	69	-14	51
24	Bristol City	46	11	8	27	59	84	-25	41

MANAGERS OF THE MONTH

August: Ian Holloway (Blackpool)
September: Dougie Freedman (Crystal Palace)
October: Tony Mowbray (Middlesbrough)
November: Kenny Jackett (Millwall)
December: Steve Bruce (Hull City)
January: Nigel Pearson (Leicester City)
February: Gianfranco Zola (Watford)
March: Billy Davies (Nottingham Forest)
April: Dougie Freedman (Bolton Wanderers)

PFA TEAM OF THE YEAR

Kasper Schmeichel (Leicester City),
Kieran Trippier (Burnley), **Wes Morgan**
(Leicester City), **Mark Hudson** (Cardiff City),
Wayne Bridge (Brighton), **Wilfried Zaha**
(Crystal Palace), **Thomas Ince** (Blackpool),
Peter Whittingham (Cardiff City),
Yannick Bolasie (Crystal Palace),
Glenn Murray (Crystal Palace),
Matej Vydra (Watford)

LEAGUE ONE
FINAL TABLE 2012-13

A dramatic final day of the season saw Doncaster Rovers return to the Championship at the first attempt and Brentford miss out on automatic promotion.

With seconds remaining of the final game it was goal less at Brentford's Griffin Park and Rovers looked like sealing their promotion – then the home side were awarded a penalty.

Marcello Trotta took the spot-kick and hit the crossbar. The ball bounced into play, Billy Paynter slotted it to James Coppinger and he struck the winner for Doncaster.

That not only sealed promotion but also put Donny above Bournemouth for the title. Brentford had to settle for the play-offs.

The play-off semi-finals saw Brentford beat Swindon and Yeovil eliminate Sheffield United.

Yeovil had a 2-0 lead at half time in the final and despite conceding just six minutes into the second 45 minutes hung on for victory. They are now in the second-flight for the first time.

TOP SCORERS

- **23** **Paddy Madden** (Yeovil Town)
- **19** **Brett Pitman** (Bournemouth), **Leon Clarke** (Coventry City) and **Will Grigg** (Walsall)
- **18** **Clayton Donaldson** (Brentford)
- **16** **David McGoldrick** (Coventry City) and **Kevin Lisbie** (Leyton Orient)
- **14** **James Collins** (Swindon Town) and **James Hayter** (Yeovil Town)
- **13** **Lewis Grabban** (Bournemouth), **Matt Ritchie** (Bournemouth) **Billy Paynter** (Doncaster) and **Jose Baxter** (Oldham)

Kevin Lisbie, Leyton Orient

2013

POS	TEAM	P	W	D	L	F	A	GD	PTS
1	Doncaster Rovers	46	25	9	12	62	44	18	84
2	Bournemouth	46	24	11	11	76	53	23	83
3	Brentford	46	21	16	9	62	47	15	79
4	Yeovil Town	46	23	8	15	71	56	15	77
5	Sheffield United	46	19	18	9	56	42	14	75
6	Swindon Town	46	20	14	12	72	39	33	74
7	Leyton Orient	46	21	8	17	55	48	7	71
8	MK Dons	46	19	13	14	62	45	17	70
9	Walsall	46	17	17	12	65	58	7	68
10	Crawley Town	46	18	14	14	59	58	1	68
11	Tranmere	46	19	10	17	58	48	10	67
12	Notts County	46	16	17	13	61	49	12	65
13	Crewe	46	18	10	18	54	62	-8	64
14	Preston North End	46	14	17	15	54	49	5	59
*15	Coventry City	46	18	11	17	66	59	7	55
16	Shrewsbury	46	13	16	17	54	60	-6	55
17	Carlisle United	46	14	13	19	56	77	-21	55
18	Stevenage	46	15	9	22	47	64	-17	54
19	Oldham Athletic	46	14	9	23	46	59	-13	51
20	Colchester United	46	14	9	23	47	68	-21	51
R21	Scunthorpe United	46	13	9	24	49	73	-24	48
R22	Bury	46	9	14	23	45	73	-28	41
R23	Hartlepool United	46	9	14	23	39	67	-28	41
*R24	Portsmouth	46	10	12	24	51	69	-18	32

*Ten points deducted

MANAGERS OF THE MONTH

August: Ronnie Moore (Tranmere Rovers)
September: Ronnie Moore (Tranmere Rovers)
October: Danny Wilson (Sheffield United)
November: Eddie Howe (Bournemouth)
December: Mark Robins (Coventry City)
January: Dean Smith (Walsall)
February: John Hughes (Hartlepool United)
March: Russell Slade (Leyton Orient)
April: Eddie Howe (Bournemouth)

PFA TEAM OF THE YEAR

Wes Foderingham (Swindon Town),
Simon Francis (Bournemouth), **Rob Jones**
(Doncaster Rovers), **Harry Maguire**
(Sheffield United), **Charlie Daniels**
(Bournemouth), **Matt Ritchie** (Bournemouth),
Luke Murphy (Crewe Alexandra), **Alan Judge**
(Notts County), **David Cotterill**
(Doncaster Rovers), **Paddy Madden**
(Yeovil Town), **Leon Clarke** (Coventry City).

Gillingham were already confirmed as League
Two champions going into the final weekend of the season.

But the last day's games resulted in both Aldershot Town and Barnet dropped out of the Football League and back into the Conference.

The Gills' victory was the first promotion achieved by boss Martin Allen, despite 17 mostly successful years as a football manager.

The play-off semi-finals saw Bradford City elminate Burton Albion and Northampton Town brush past Cheltenham Town.

In the final, Bradford hit three goals in the first half hour to beat Northampton 3-0 and make up for their League Cup Final defeat at Wembley earlier in the season.

Nahki Wells, Bradford City

TOP SCORERS

31 **Tom Pope** (Port Vale)

21 **Jamie Cureton** (Exeter City)

18 **Nahki Wells** (Bradford City) and **Daniel Nardiello** (Rotherham)

16 **Adebayo Akinfenwa** (Northampton), **Rene Howe** (Torquay)

15 **Jacques Maghoma** (Burton), **Jack Redshaw** (Morecambe), **Bobby Grant** (Rochdale) and **Britt Assombalonga** (Southend)

Tom Pope, Port Vale

2013

POS	TEAM	P	W	D	L	F	A	GD	PTS
1	Gillingham	46	23	14	9	66	39	27	83
2	Rotherham United	46	24	7	15	74	59	15	79
3	Port Vale	46	21	15	10	87	52	35	78
4	Burton Albion	46	22	10	14	71	65	6	76
5	Cheltenham Town	46	20	15	11	58	51	7	75
6	Northampton Town	46	21	10	15	64	55	9	73
7	Bradford City	46	18	15	13	63	52	11	69
8	Chesterfield	46	18	13	15	60	45	15	67
9	Oxford United	46	19	8	19	60	61	-1	65
10	Exeter City	46	18	10	18	63	62	1	64
11	Southend United	46	16	13	17	61	55	6	61
12	Rochdale	46	16	13	17	68	70	-2	61
13	Fleetwood Town	46	15	15	16	55	57	-2	60
14	Bristol Rovers	46	16	12	18	60	69	-9	60
15	Wycombe Wanderers	46	17	9	20	50	60	-10	60
16	Morecambe	46	15	13	18	55	61	-6	58
17	York City	46	12	19	15	50	60	-10	55
18	Accrington Stanley	46	14	12	20	51	68	-17	54
19	Torquay United	46	13	14	19	55	62	-7	53
20	AFC Wimbledon	46	14	11	21	54	76	-22	53
21	Plymouth Argle	46	13	13	20	46	55	-9	52
22	Dagenham & Redbridge	46	13	12	21	55	62	-7	51
23	Barnet	46	13	12	21	47	59	-12	51
24	Aldershot Town	46	11	15	20	42	60	-18	48

MANAGERS OF THE MONTH

August: Martin Allen (Gillingham)
September: Micky Adams (Port Vale)
October: Mark Yates (Cheltenham)
November: Paul Sturrock (Southend)
December: Gary Rowett (Burton Albion)
January: Martin Allen (Gillingham)
February: Gary Rowett (Burton Albion)
March: John Sheridan (Plymouth)
April: Nigel Worthington (York City)

PFA TEAM OF THE YEAR

Stuart Nelson (Gillingham),
Sean Clohessy (Southend United),
Adam Barrett (Gillingham), **Ryan Cresswell**
(Southend United), **Joe Martin** (Gillingham),
Jacques Maghoma (Burton Albion),
Marlon Pack (Cheltenham Town), **Gary Jones**
(Bradford City), **Jennison Myrie-Williams**
(Port Vale), **Tom Pope** (Port Vale),
Jamie Cureton (Exeter City)

CONFERENCE
FINAL TABLE 2012-13

Champions Mansfield Town returned to the Football League after a five-year absence. In the play-off semi-finals Wrexham beat Kidderminster Harriers and Newport County defeated Grimsby. Newport won 2-0 against Wrexham in the final to end a 25-year exile from the League.

2013

POS	TEAM	P	W	D	L	F	A	GD	PTS
1	Mansfield Town	46	30	5	11	92	52	40	95
2	Kidderminster Harriers	46	28	9	9	82	40	42	93
3	Newport County AFC	46	25	10	11	85	60	25	85
4	Grimsby Town	46	23	14	9	70	38	32	83
5	Wrexham	46	22	14	10	74	45	29	80
6	Hereford United	46	19	13	14	73	63	10	70
7	Luton Town	46	18	13	15	70	62	8	67
8	Dartford	46	19	9	18	67	63	4	66
9	Braintree Town	46	19	9	18	63	72	9	66
10	Forest Green Rovers	46	18	11	17	63	49	14	65
11	Macclesfield Town	46	17	12	17	65	70	5	63
12	Woking	46	18	8	20	73	81	8	62
13	Alfreton Town	46	16	12	18	69	74	5	60
14	Cambridge United	46	15	14	17	68	69	1	59
15	Nuneaton	46	14	15	17	55	63	8	57
16	Lincoln City	46	15	11	20	66	73	7	56
17	Gateshead	46	13	16	17	58	61	3	55
18	Hyde FC	46	16	7	23	63	75	12	55
19	Tamworth	46	15	10	21	55	69	14	55
20	Southport	46	14	12	20	72	86	14	54
21	Stockport County	46	13	11	22	57	76	19	50
22	Barrow	46	11	13	22	45	83	38	46
23	Ebbsfleet United	46	8	15	23	55	89	34	39
24	Telford United	46	6	17	23	52	79	27	35

SCOTTISH PREMIER LEAGUE FINAL TABLE 2012-13

There was no big shock at the top of the SPL – with Celtic walking away with their 44th title. With Rangers demoted to the bottom division following their financial problems it was more a case of which teams could try to cash in on the extra European places available to the top three sides.

POS	TEAM	P	W	D	L	F	A	GD	PTS
C 1	**Celtic**	38	24	7	7	92	35	57	79
2	**Motherwell**	38	18	9	11	67	51	16	63
3	**St. Johnstone**	38	14	14	10	45	44	1	56
4	**Inverness CT**	38	13	15	10	64	60	4	54
5	**Ross County**	38	13	14	11	47	48	-1	53
6	**Dundee United**	38	11	14	13	51	62	-11	47
7	**Hibernian**	38	13	12	13	49	52	-3	51
8	**Aberdeen**	38	11	15	12	41	43	-2	48
9	**Kilmarnock**	38	11	12	15	52	53	-1	45
10	**Hearts**	38	11	11	16	40	49	-9	44
11	**St. Mirren**	38	9	14	15	47	60	-13	41
R 12	**Dundee**	38	7	9	22	28	66	-38	30

TOP SCORERS

26 **Michael Higdon** (Motherwell)
23 **Leigh Griffiths** (Hibs),
Billy McKay (Inverness)
20 **Niall McGinn** (Aberdeen)
19 **Gary Hooper** (Celtic)
Johnny Russell (Dundee United),
13 **Steven Thompson** (St. Mirren)
12 **Andrew Shinnie** (Inverness)
11 **Kriss Commons** (Celtic)
10 **Jon Daley** (Dundee United), **Eoin Doyle** (Hibs), **Jamie Murphy** (Ross County)

MANAGERS OF THE MONTH

August: Derek Adams (Ross County)
September: Steve Lomas (St. Johnstone)
October: Craig Brown (Aberdeen)
November: Terry Butcher (Inverness CT)
December: Neil Lennon (Celtic)
January: Derek Adams (Ross County)
February: Derek Adams (Ross County)
March: Stuart McCall (Motherwell)
April: John Brown (Dundee)
Manager of the Year:
Stuart McCall (Motherwell)

SCOTTISH
FIRST DIVISION

Partick Thistle went up as champions and Airdrie United were relegated.

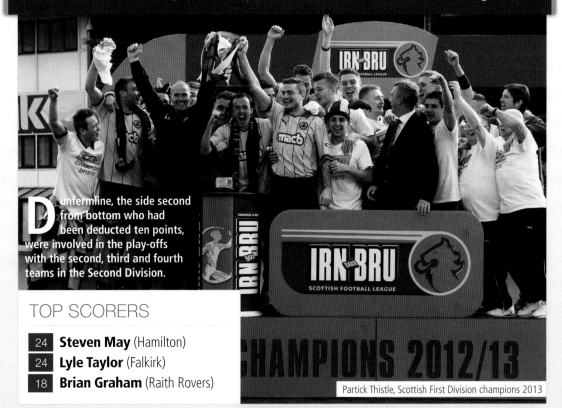

Dunfermline, the side second from bottom who had been deducted ten points, were involved in the play-offs with the second, third and fourth teams in the Second Division.

TOP SCORERS

24	**Steven May** (Hamilton)
24	**Lyle Taylor** (Falkirk)
18	**Brian Graham** (Raith Rovers)

Partick Thistle, Scottish First Division champions 2013

POS	TEAM	P	W	D	L	GD	PTS
1	**Partick Thistle**	36	23	9	4	48	78
2	**Morton**	36	20	7	9	26	67
3	**Falkirk**	36	15	8	13	4	53
4	**Livingston**	36	14	10	12	2	53
5	**Hamilton Academical**	36	14	9	13	7	51
6	**Raith Rovers**	36	11	13	12	-3	46
7	**Dumbarton**	36	13	4	19	-25	43
8	**Cowdenbeath**	36	8	12	16	-14	36
*9	**Dunfermline Athletic**	36	14	7	15	3	34
10	**Airdrie United**	36	5	7	24	-48	22

*Ten points deducted

SCOTTISH SECOND DIVISION

Queen of the South went up as champions. With Alloa, Brechin City and Forfar meeting Dunfermline of the First Division in the play-offs.

n the two-legged semi-finals Dunfermline beat Forfar and Alloa defeated Brechin City. The final saw Alloa beat Dunfermline 3-1 over two legs.

Albion Rovers were relegated automatically and second bottom side East Fife were in the play-offs with the second, third and fourth teams in the Third Division.

POS	TEAM	P	W	D	L	GD	PTS
1	Queen of the South	36	29	5	2	69	92
2	Alloa Athletic	36	20	7	9	27	67
3	Brechin City	36	19	4	13	13	61
4	Forfar Athletic	36	17	3	16	-7	54
5	Arbroath	36	15	7	14	-10	52
6	Stenhousemuir	36	12	13	11	0	49
7	Ayr United	36	12	5	19	-12	41
8	Stranraer	36	10	7	19	-28	37
9	East Fife	36	8	8	11	-15	32
10	Albion Rovers	36	7	3	26	-37	24

TOP SCORERS

32 **Nick Clark** (Queen of the South)

18 **John Gemmell** (Stenhousemuir)

18 **Craig Malcolm** (Stranraer)

SCOTTISH THIRD DIVISION

Rangers went up as champions with Peterhead, Queen's Park and Berwick Rangers involved in the play-offs with East Fife from the Second Division.

n the semi-finals East Fife beat Berwick over two legs and Peterhead defeated Queen's Park. The two-legged final was won 1-0 by East Fife.

East Stirlingshire remain in the league despite finishing bottom.

POS	TEAM	P	W	D	L	GD	PTS
1	Rangers	36	25	8	3	58	83
2	Peterhead	36	17	8	11	24	59
3	Queen's Park	36	16	8	12	6	56
4	Berwick Rangers	36	14	7	15	4	49
5	Elgin City	36	13	10	13	-2	49
6	Montrose	36	12	11	13	-8	47
7	Stirling Albion	36	12	9	15	1	45
8	Annan Athletic	36	11	10	15	-11	43
9	Clyde	36	12	4	20	-24	40
10	East Stirlingshire	36	8	5	23	-48	29

TOP SCORERS

22 **Andrew Little** (Rangers)

21 **Rory McAllister** (Peterhead)

17 **Darren Lavery** (Berwick) and **Lee McCulloch** (Rangers)

LEAGUE LEADERS

England's Football League was the first domestic competition of its kind and in 2013 celebrated 125 years' of existence. Here's when other leagues were formed around the world…

1888	England		1936	USSR
1890	Ireland, Scotland, Holland		1937	Norway, Haiti
1891	Argentina		1938	Portugal
1895	Belgium		1943	Mexico
1897	Switzerland		1948	Colombia
1900	Uruguay		1956	Ghana
1901	Hungary		1957	Ecuador
1906	Paraguay		1959	Brazil, Turkey
1909	Romania		1960	Ivory Coast
1911	Austria		1962	Algeria, Zambia
1912	Peru		1963	Germany
1921	USA, Ireland, Tunisia and Venezuela		1965	Japan
1924	Sweden, Bulgaria		1966	Mali, Nigeria
1925	Czechoslovakia (1993: Czech Republic and Slovakia)		1977	Australia, Bolivia
1927	Greece		1983	South Korea
1929	Spain, Italy and Denmark		1988	Panama
1932	France		1992	Croatia, Ukraine
1933	Chile		2000	Bosnia
			2001	Russia
			2006	Montenegro, Serbia

RED
DOMINATION

HOW MANCHESTER UNITED REACHED

20 ENGLISH
TITLE WINS

Manchester United's 2012-13 Premier League victory was Sir Alex Ferguson's 13th title as their manager. That made it a staggering 20 titles for the club, an English best. Here's how the Red Devils notched up that silverware...

DIVISION ONE

1952

Sir Matt Busby's was in charge as the Red Devils finished four points clear of both Tottenham and Arsenal.

1957

Busby's side retained the title and completed a hat-trick of wins for the boss. Tottenham and Preston were both eight points short.

1908

Ernest Mangnall was the Red Devils' manager and United finished nine points clear of rivals Manchester City and Aston Villa.

1956

Another title for Busby, this time 11 points ahead of runners-up Blackpool and third-placed Wolves.

1965

Just goal difference pushed Leeds United into second. Chelsea were five points off the pace in third.

1911

Mangnall was still in the gaffer's hotseat as United beat Villa by just one point. Sunderland were third, a further seven points adrift of the champions.

1967

Golden boy George Best, the Northern Ireland forward, lifted his second title with United. Nottingham Forest and Tottenham were both four points behind the winners.

THE FERGIE ERA

1996

Pundits said United couldn't win with kids. But Fergie's Fledglings were four points ahead of Newcastle. Cantona returned from his kung-fu ban.

1999

Just one point put United ahead of Arsenal. The Red Devils also lifted the FA and European cups, inspired by Teddy Sheringham.

1993

Sir Alex Ferguson's first English title in the debut season of the Premiership. United were ten points clear of Aston Villa as Eric Cantona strutted his stuff.

1997

Ole Gunnar Solskjaer, the 'baby faced assassin', was top scorer for United with 18 as they beat Newcastle by seven points.

2000

An amazing 18 points separated United and Arsenal. Dwight Yorke rattled the net with 20 goals.

1994

Bryan Robson captained the club as they collected a staggering 92 points to beat Blackburn on 84 — the same total that had won the crown for Fergie the previous season.

2001

Defender Gary Neville made the most appearances — 32 — as Sir Alex made it three in a row. The champions were ten points ahead of Arsenal and 11 in front of Liverpool.

2003

Holland hitman Ruud van Nistelrooy struck 25 league goals – 44 in total – to leave Arsenal five points adrift. Newcastle were a further nine behind in third.

2009

United equaled Liverpool's record of 18 English titles as Fergie collected his 11th victory in the competition. Giggs also created a new individual best with his 11th title.

2007

Ron and Roon formed the R Team! The 31 goals from the partnership of Cristiano Ronaldo and Wayne Rooney helped put United six points clear of Chelsea, and a further five ahead of Liverpool.

2011

United became English football's record title-winners. Dimitar Berbatov struck 20 league goals as United finished nine points ahead of Chelsea and Manchester City.

2008

Ronaldo collected the Golden Boot thanks to his 31 league goals. His last of the season, plus one from Ryan Giggs, gave them a final day 2-0 win at Wigan that clinched the title.

2013

A 3-0 victory over Aston Villa sealed United's 20th title – all the goals scored by their No.20, £24m Robin van Persie. With four games still to play Fergie's side had the title in the bag.

Crowded House

THE BEST HOME ATTENDANCES IN THE PREMIER LEAGUE 2012-13

TOTAL GATES

1.	**Manchester United** 1,435,063	
2.	**Arsenal** 1,141,507	
3.	**Newcastle** 959,826	
4.	**Manchester City** 892,506	
5.	**Liverpool** 850,224	
6.	**Chelsea** 787,786	
7.	**Sunderland** 770,344	
8.	**Everton** 690,763	
9.	**Tottenham** 685,266	
10.	**Aston Villa** 666,135	
11.	**West Ham** 659,677	
12.	**Southampton** 586,602	
13.	**Stoke City** 511,467	
14.	**Norwich City** 506,762	
15.	**Fulham** 482,492	
16.	**West Brom** 481,838	
17.	**Reading** 453,378	
18.	**Swansea City** 387,037	
19.	**Wigan Athletic** 345,126	
20.	**QPR** 337,808	

Arsenal
Best: v Manchester United, 60,112
Average: 60,079

QPR
Best: v Man United, 18,337
Average: 17,779

Aston Villa
Best: v Chelsea 42,084
Average: 35,059

Reading
Best: v Everton, 24,184
Average: 23,862

Chelsea
Best: v Man City, 41,792
Average: 41,462

Southampton
Best: v Liverpool, 32,070
Average: 30,873

Everton
Best: v Liverpoool 39,613
Average: 36,355

Stoke City
Best: v Aston Villa, 27, 544
Average: 26,919

Fulham
Best: v Southampton, Swansea and Arsenal, 25,700 **Average:** 25,394

Sunderland
Best: v Newcastle, 47, 456
Average: 40,544

Liverpool
Best: v Chelsea 45,009
Average: 44,748

Swansea City
Best: v Man United, 20,650
Average: 20,370

Manchester City
Best: v Everton 47,386
Average: 46,974

Tottenham
Best: v Sunderland 36,763
Average: 36,066

Manchester United
Best: v Reading 75,605
Average: 75,529

West Brom
Best: v Man United, 26,438
Average: 25,359

Newcastle United
Best: v Tottenham, 52,385
Average: 50,517

West Ham
Best: v Man City, Stoke, Chelsea, Liverpool, Everton, Norwich, Spurs, 35,005 **Average:** 34,719

Norwich City
Best: v Aston Villa, 26,842
Average: 26,671

Wigan Athletic
Best: v Tottenham, 22,326
Average: 19,173

The Best
Crowds Ever

THE RECORD ATTENDANCES FOR ALL OF THE CURRENT ENGLISH PREMIER AND FOOTBALL LEAGUE CLUBS

Accrington Stanley:
13,181 v Hull City, Third Division (North), 1948
AFC Bournemouth:
28,799 v Manchester United, FA Cup, 1957
AFC Wimbledon:
4,749 v Exeter City, League Two, 2013
Arsenal:
73,295 v Sunderland, Division 1, 1935
Aston Villa:
76,588 v Derby, FA Cup, 1947
Barnsley:
42,255 v Stoke City, FA Cup, 1936
Birmingham City:
66,844 v Everton, FA Cup, 1939
Blackburn Rovers:
62,522 v Bolton, FA Cup, 1929
Blackpool:
38,098 v Wolves, Division One, 1955
Bolton Wanderers:
69,912 v Manchester City, FA Cup, 1933
Bradford City:
39,146 v Burnley, FA Cup, 1911
Brentford:
38,678 v Leicester City, FA Cup, 1949
Brighton and Hove Albion:
36,747 v Fulham Division 2, 1958
Bristol City:
43,335 v Preston, FA Cup, 1935
Bristol Rovers:
38,472 v Preston North End, FA Cup, 1960
Burnley:
54,775 v Huddersfield Town, FA Cup, 1924
Burton Albion:
6,192 v Oxford United, Conference, 2009
Bury:
35,000 v Bolton Wanderers, FA Cup, 1960
Cardiff City:
57,893 v Arsenal Division 1, 1953
Carlisle United:
27,500 v Birmingham City, FA Cup, 1957 and v Middlesbrough, FA Cup, 1970

Charlton Athletic:
75,031 v Aston Villa, FA Cup, 1938
Chelsea:
82,905 v Arsenal, Division 1, 1935
Cheltenham Town:
10,389 v Blackpool, FA Cup, 1934
Chesterfield:
30,968 v Newcastle United, Second Division, 1939
Colchester United:
19,072 v Reading, FA Cup, 1948
Coventry City:
51,455 v Wolves, Second Division, 1967
Crawley Town:
5,880 v Reading, FA Cup, 2013
Crewe Alexandra:
20,000 v Tottenham, FA Cup, 1960
Crystal Palace:
51,482 v Burnley, Division 2, 1979
Dagenham & Redbridge:
4,791 v Shrewsbury Town, League Two, 2009
Derby County:
41,826 v Tottenham, Division One, 1969
Doncaster Rovers:
37,149 v Hull City, Third Division (North), 1948
Everton:
78,299 v Liverpool, Division 1, 1948
Exeter City:
20,984 v Sunderland, FA Cup, 1931
Fleetwood Town:
6,150 v Rochdale, FA Cup, 1997
Fulham:
49,335 v Millwall, Division Two, 1938
Gillingham:
23,002 v QPR, FA Cup, 1948
Hartlepool United:
17,426 v Manchester United, FA Cup, 1957
Huddersfield Town:
67,037 v Arsenal, FA Cup, 1932
Hull City:
55,019 v Manchester United, FA Cup, 1949

Ipswich Town:
38,010 v Leeds United, FA Cup, 1975
Leeds United:
57,892 v Sunderland FA Cup, 1967
Leicester City:
47,298, Tottenham, FA Cup, 1928
Leyton Orient:
34,345 v West Ham United, FA Cup, 1964
Liverpool:
61,905 v Wolves, FA Cup, 1952
Manchester City:
84,569 v Stoke City, FA Cup, 1934
Manchester United:
76,098 v Blackburn, Premier League, 2007
Mansfield Town:
24,467 v Nottingham Forest, FA Cup, 1953
Middlesbrough:
53,596 v Newcastle United, Division One, 1949
Millwall:
48,762 v Derby County, FA Cup, 1937
Milton Keynes Dons:
19,506 v QPR, FA Cup, 2012
Morecambe:
9,383 v Weymouth, FA Cup, 1962
Newcastle United:
68,386 v Chelsea, Division One, 1930
Newport County:
24,268 v Cardiff City, Third Division (South), 1937
Northampton Town:
24,523 v Fulham, First Division, 1965
Norwich City:
43,984 v Leicester City, FA Cup, 1963
Nottingham Forest:
49,946 v Man United, Division One, 1967
Notts County:
47,310 v York City, FA Cup, 1955
Oldham Athletic:
46,471 v Sheffield Wednesday, FA Cup, 1930
Oxford United:
22,750 v Preston, FA Cup, 1964
Peterborough United:
30,096 v Swansea Town, FA Cup, 1965
Plymouth Argyle:
43,596 v Aston Villa, Second Division, 1936
Port Vale:
49, 768 v Aston Villa, FA Cup, 1960
Portsmouth:
51,358 v Derby County, FA Cup, 1949
Preston North End:
42,684 v Arsenal, First Division, 1938
Queens Park Rangers:
35,353 v Leeds United, Division One, 1974

Reading:
24,160 v Tottenham, Premier League, 2012
Rochdale:
24,231 v Notts County, FA Cup, 1949
Rotherham United:
25,170 v Sheffield United, Second Division, 1952
Scunthorpe United:
23,935 v Portsmouth, FA Cup, 1954
Sheffield United:
68,287 v Leeds United, FA Cup, 1936
Sheffield Wednesday:
72,841 v Manchester City, FA Cup, 1934
Shrewsbury Town:
18,917 v Walsall, Third Division, 1961
Southampton:
32,363 v Coventry City, Championship, 2012
Southend United:
31,090 v Liverpool, FA Cup, 1979
Stevenage:
8,040 v Arsenal, FA Cup, 1998
Stoke City:
28,218 v Everton, FA Cup, 2002
Sunderland:
48,335 v Liverpool, Premier League, 2002
Swansea City:
20,650 v Manchester United, Premier League, 2012
Swindon Town:
32,000 v Arsenal, FA Cup, 1997
Torquay United:
21,908 v Huddersfield Town, FA Cup, 1955
Tottenham Hotspur:
75,038 v Sunderland, FA Cup, 1938
Tranmere Rovers:
24,424 v Stoke City, FA Cup, 1972
Walsall:
25,453 v Newcastle United, Second Division, 1961
Watford:
34,099 v Manchester United, FA Cup, 1969
West Bromwich Albion:
64,815 v Arsenal, FA Cup, 1937
West Ham United:
42,322 v Tottenham, Division One, 1970
Wigan Athletic:
25,133 v Man United, Premier League, 2008
Wolverhampton Wanderers:
61,315 v Liverpool, FA Cup, 1939
Wycombe Wanderers:
15,850 v St Albans City, FA Amateur Cup, 1950
Yeovil Town:
16,318 v Sunderland, FA Cup, 1949
York City:
28,123 v Huddersfield Town, FA Cup, 1938

Premier Bosse

Pay League

I t's a well-paid job but being a football club manager can also be one of the most insecure posts around.

They might not be in the same league as players when it comes to collecting cash, but the bigger bosses arent short of a few quid in the bank.

It will come as no surprise that the Premier League's longest-serving and most successful manager – Sir Alex Ferguson at Manchester United – is also top of the pile financially. He certainly won't struggle like most pensioners now he has finally retired.

And there are a number of other managers wh worked in the top-flight – or who are still there – won't be going short when they hang up the tra

Here are the richest football managers, who ha been based in the UK and Ireland, the team they currently working with or the sides they managed

Oh, and the experts reckon that these guys cou actually be worth a lot more than these figures a financial wizards don't know how much cash the bosses have in the bank.

1   Sir Alex Ferguson
(ex-Manchester United) £34m

2= Roy Keane
(ex-Ipswich) £29m

2= Arsene Wenger
(Arsenal) £29m

4= Roberto Mancini
(ex-Manchester City) £21m

4= Giovanni Trapattoni
(Republic of Ireland) £21m

6 Sven Goran Eriksson
(ex-Leicester City) £16m

7= Steve Bruce
(Hull City) £14m

7= Mark Hughes
(Stoke City) £14m

9 Harry Redknapp
(QPR) £13m

10= Rafa Benitez
(now Napoli) £12m

10= Roy Hodgson
(England) £12m

10= Martin O'Neill
(ex-Sunderland) £12m

PREMIER BOSSES SACKED IN 2012-13

Roberto Di Matteo (Chelsea)
Mark Hughes (QPR)
Brian McDermott (Reading)
Martin O'Neill (Sunderland)
Nigel Adkins (Southampton)
Tony Pulis (Stoke City)
Roberto Mancini (Man City)

ROVER AND OUT...

Blackburn Rovers didn't hang on to managers for very long during 2012-13! Steve Kean was in charge at the start of the season in August but was dismissed the following month.

Assistant manager Eric Black took over for six games as caretaker boss before former defender Henning Berg became gaffer for ten games in 57 days before he was on his way out of Ewood Park.

Reserve team boss Gary Bowyer looked after the team temporarily for four matches before Michael Appleton arrived as the next permanent boss. He lasted 15 games in 67 days.

Bowyer was then reinstated as caretaker manager.

Premier
Pay League

Former England captain David Beckham is one of – if not THE – richest footballers in the world.

It's estimated that his playing contracts and deals with the likes of adidas and other sponsors have put around £165m in the bank.

And don't forget that Mrs Beckham – Victoria Posh Spice – isn't short of a few quid either!

The highest paid Premier League players include Chelsea's Eden Hazard on a reported £185,000 a week; Wayne Rooney, Robin van Persie, Yaya Toure and Carlos Tevez, all thought to pick up £180,000 every seven days!

Here are the top twenty richest top-flight stars at the end of 2012-13, according to the

1	**Wayne Rooney**
	(Manchester United) £51m

2	Rio Ferdinand
	(Manchester United) £42m

3	Michael Owen
	(Stoke City) £38m

4	Ryan Giggs
	(Manchester United) £34m

5	Frank Lampard
	(Chelsea) £34m

6	Steven Gerrard
	(Liverpool) £33m

7	Fernando Torres
	(Chelsea) £28m

8	John Terry
	(Chelsea) £24m

9	Joe Cole
	(West Ham) £21m

10	Petr Cech
	(Chelsea) £20m

11	Paul Scholes
	(Manchester United) £19m

12=	Ashley Cole
	(Chelsea) £18m

12=	Damien Duff
	(Fulham) £18m

12=	Carlos Tevez
	(Manchester City) £18m

15	Yaya Toure
	(Manchester City) £17m

16	Jamie Carragher
	(Liverpool) £16m

17=	Dimitar Berbatov
	(Fulham) £15m

17=	Ji-Sung Park
	(QPR) £15m

17=	David Silva
	(Manchester City) £15m

20=	Emanuel Adebayor
	(Tottenham) £14m

20=	Sergio Aguero
	(Manchester City) £14m

MANAGER
OF THE SEASON

The Premier League Manager of the Season award started in the second campaign of the competition and the first winner was Manchester United's Sir Alex Ferguson after guiding his side to a second successive title.

2011-12

ALL THE WINNERS...

1993-94	Alex Ferguson (Manchester United)
1994-95	Kenny Dalglish (Blackburn Rovers)
1995-96	Alex Ferguson (Manchester United)
1996-97	Alex Ferguson (Manchester United)
1997-98	Arsene Wenger (Arsenal)
1998-99	Alex Ferguson (Manchester United)
1999-00	Alex Ferguson (Manchester United)
2000-01	George Burley (Ipswich Town)
2001-02	Arsene Wenger (Arsenal)
2002-03	Alex Ferguson (Manchester United)
2003-04	Arsene Wenger (Arsenal)
2004-05	Jose Mourinho (Chelsea)
2005-06	Jose Mourinho (Chelsea)
2006-07	Alex Ferguson (Manchester United)

2007-08	Alex Ferguson (Manchester United)
2008-09	Alex Ferguson (Manchester United)
2009-10	Harry Redknapp (Tottenham)
2010-11	Alex Ferguson (Manchester United)
2011-12	Alan Pardew (Newcastle United)
2012-13	Alex Ferguson (Manchester United)

2012-13

2009-10

MANAGER
OF THE MONTH

The Premier League Manager of the Month award started in August 1993 and the first one went to Sir Alex Ferguson at Manchester United. Until the end of season 2012-13 some 32 managers have won the award more than once:

27 Alex Ferguson (Manchester United)
12 Arsene Wenger (Arsenal)
10 David Moyes (Everton)
8 Martin O'Neill (Leicester, Aston Villa, Sunderland)
8 Harry Redknapp (West Ham, Portsmouth, Southampton, Tottenham, QPR)
6 Bobby Robson (Newcastle United)
6 Rafael Benitez (Liverpool, Chelsea)
5 Kevin Keegan (Newcastle United)
4 Sam Allardyce (Bolton, West Ham)
4 Carlo Ancelotti (Chelsea)
4 Roy Hodgson (Blackburn Rovers, Fulham)
4 Joe Kinnear (Wimbledon)
4 Gordon Strachan (Coventry, Southampton)
3 Alan Curbishley (Charlton)
3 Gerard Houllier (Liverpool)
3 Jose Mourinho (Chelsea)
3 David O'Leary (Leeds)
3 Stuart Pearce (Nottingham Forest, Manchester City)
2 Frank Clark (Nottingham Forest)
2 Steve Coppell (Reading)
2 Kenny Dalglish (Blackburn Rovers)
2 Roy Evans (Liverpool)
2 John Gregory (Aston Villa)
2 Glenn Hoddle (Tottenham)
2 Paul Jewell (Wigan)
2 Roberto Mancini (Manchester City)
2 Owen Coyle (Bolton)
2 Claudio Ranieri (Chelsea)
2 Peter Reid (Sunderland)
2 Graeme Souness (Southampton)
2 Phil Thomson (Liverpool)
2 Andre Villas-Boas (Tottenham)

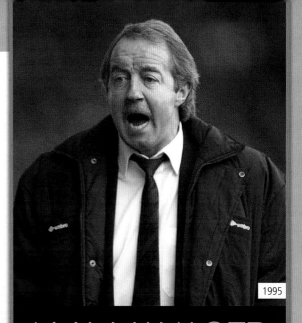

1995

LMA MANAGER
OF THE YEAR

The League Managers' Association also hand out an award to their boss of the year. It is voted for by other managers.

1994 Joe Kinnear (Wimbledon)
1995 Frank Clark (Nottingham Forest)
1996 Peter Reid (Sunderland)
1997 Danny Wilson (Barnsley)
1998 Dave Jones (Southampton)
1999 Alex Ferguson (Manchester United)
2000 Alan Curbishley (Charlton)
2001 George Burley (Ipswich Town)
2002 Arsene Wenger (Arsenal)
2003 David Moyes (Everton)
2004 Arsene Wenger (Arsenal)
2005 David Moyes (Everton)
2006 Steve Coppell (Reading)
2007 Steve Coppell (Reading)
2008 Alex Ferguson (Manchester United)
2009 David Moyes (Everton)
2010 Roy Hodgson (Fulham)
2011 Alex Ferguson (Manchester United)
2012 Alan Pardew (Newcastle United)
2013 Alex Ferguson (Manchester United)

WORLD PLAYER OF THE YEAR

Since 1991 coaches and captains of international teams have voted for their World Player of the Year.

In 2010 this award was merged with the Ballon d'Or to create one award, the FIFA Ballon d'Or.

Barcelona and Argentina forward Lionel Messi has won the prestigious accolade for an unprecedented FOUR consecutive years!

2012
Lionel Messi
Argentina,
Barcelona

2011
Lionel Messi
Argentina,
Barcelona

2010
Lionel Messi
Argentina,
Barcelona

2009
Lionel Messi
Argentina,
Barcelona

2008
Cristiano Ronaldo
Portugal,
Manchester United

2007
Kaka
Brazil,
AC Milan

2006
Fabio Cannavaro
Italy, Real Madrid

2005
Ronaldinho
Brazil,
Barcelona

2004
Ronaldinho
Brazil,
Barcelona

1997
Ronaldo
Brazil, Inter Milan

2003
Zinedine
Zidane
France, Real Madrid

1996
Ronaldo
Brazil, Barcelona

2002
Ronaldo
Brazil,
Real Madrid

1995
George
Weah
Liberia, AC Milan

2001
Luis Figo
Portugal,
Real Madrid

1994
Romario
Brazil,
Barcelona

2000
Zinedine
Zidane
France, Juventus

1993
Roberto
Baggio
Italy, Juventus

1999
Rivaldo
Brazil,
Barcelona

1992
Marco
van Basten
Holland, AC Milan

1998
Zinedine
Zidane
France, Juventus

1991
Lothar
Mattaus
Germany,
Inter Milan

PFA
PLAYER
OF THE YEAR

2004

The Professional Footballers' Association – the players' union – has presented its Players' Player of the Year awards since 1974. All professional players get a vote.

The stunning form of Tottenham and Wales midfielder Gareth Bale won him the 2013 Player and Young Player of the Year awards. He is only the third player to win both accodlades at the same time. The others to achieve the same standard were Andy Gray in 1977 and Cristiano Ronaldo in 2007.

ALL THE WINNERS...

1974 Norman Hunter (Leeds United)
1975 Colin Todd (Derby County)
1976 Pat Jennings (Tottenham)
1977 Andy Gray (Aston Villa)
1978 Peter Shilton (Nottingham Forest)
1979 Liam Brady (Arsenal)
1980 Terry McDermott (Liverpool)
1981 John Wark (Ipswich Town)
1982 Kevin Keegan (Southampton)
1983 Kenny Dalglish (Liverpool)
1984 Ian Rush (Liverpool)
1985 Peter Reid (Everton)
1986 Gary Lineker (Everton)
1987 Clive Allen (Tottenham)
1988 John Barnes (Liverpool)

1988

1989 Mark Hughes (Manchester United)
1990 David Platt (Aston Villa)
1991 Mark Hughes (Manchester United)
1992 Gary Pallister (Manchester United)
1993 Paul McGrath (Aston Villa)
1994 Eric Cantona (Manchester United)
1995 Alan Shearer (Blackburn Rovers)
1996 Les Ferdinand (Newcastle United)
1997 Alan Shearer (Newcastle United)
1998 Dennis Bergkamp (Arsenal)
1999 David Ginola (Tottenham)
2000 Roy Keane (Manchester United)
2001 Teddy Sheringham (Manchester United)
2002 Ruud van Nistelrooy (Manchester United)
2003 Thierry Henry (Arsenal)

2004 Thierry Henry (Arsenal)
2005 John Terry (Chelsea)
2006 Steven Gerrard (Liverpool)
2007 Cristiano Ronaldo (Manchester United)
2008 Cristiano Ronaldo (Manchester United)

2008

2009 Ryan Giggs (Manchester United)
2010 Wayne Rooney (Manchester United)
2011 Gareth Bale (Tottenham)
2012 Robin van Persie (Arsenal)
2013 Gareth Bale (Tottenham)

YOUNG PLAYER OF THE YEAR

1974 Kevin Beattie (Ipswich Town)
1975 Mervyn Day (West Ham)
1976 Peter Barnes (Manchester City)
1977 Andy Gray (Aston Villa)
1978 Tony Woodcock (Nottingham Forest)
1979 Cyrille Regis (West Brom)
1980 Glenn Hoddle (Tottenham)
1981 Gary Shaw (Aston Villa)
1982 Steve Moran (Southampton)
1983 Ian Rush (Liverpool)
1984 Paul Walsh (Luton Town)
1985 Mark Hughes (Manchester United)
1986 Tony Cottee (West Ham)
1987 Tony Adams (Arsenal)
1988 Paul Gascoigne (Newcastle United)
1989 Paul Merson (Arsenal)
1990 Matt Le Tissier (Southampton)

1991 Lee Sharpe (Manchester United)
1992 Ryan Giggs (Manchester United)
1993 Ryan Giggs (Manchester United)
1994 Andy Cole (Newcastle United)
1995 Robbie Fowler (Liverpool)
1996 Robbie Fowler (Liverpool)
1997 David Beckham (Manchester United)
1998 Michael Owen (Liverpool)
1999 Nicolas Anelka (Arsenal)
2000 Harry Kewell (Leeds United)
2001 Steven Gerrard (Liverpool)
2002 Craig Bellamy (Newcastle United)
2003 Jermaine Jenas (Newcastle United)
2004 Scott Parker (Chelsea)
2005 Wayne Rooney (Manchester United)
2006 Wayne Rooney (Manchester United)
2007 Cristiano Ronaldo (Manchester United)
2008 Cesc Fabregas (Arsenal)
2009 Ashley Young (Aston Villa)
2010 James Milner (Aston Villa)
2011 Jack Wilshere (Arsenal)
2012 Kyle Walker (Tottenham)
2013 Gareth Bale (Tottenham)

2004

FWA FOOTBALLER OF THE YEAR

T he Football Writers' Association Footballer of the Year Award was created in 1947-48 at the suggestion of Charles Buchan, famed as the publisher of *Football Monthly*. He had suggested the honour be voted for by association members.

The 2013 winner was Gareth Bale, who had already won the PFA Player and Young Player of the Year awards. He was the ninth Tottenham star to pick up the trophy – the same number of players from Manchester United have also landed the award.

2013

ALL THE WINNERS...

1948 Stanley Matthews (Blackpool)
1949 Johnny Carey (Manchester United)
1950 Joe Mercer (Arsenal)
1951 Harry Johnston (Blackpool)
1952 Billy Wright (Wolves)
1953 Nat Loftholuse (Bolton)
1954 Tom Finney (Preston North End)
1955 Don Revie (Manchester City)
1956 Bert Trautmann (Manchester City)
1957 Tom Finney (Preston North End)

1958

1958 Danny Blanchflower (Tottenham)
1959 Syd Owen (Luton Town)
1960 Bill Slater (Wolves)
1961 Danny Blanchflower (Tottenham)
1962 Jimmy Adamson (Burnley)
1963 Stanley Matthews (Stoke City)
1964 Bobby Moore (West Ham)
1965 Bobby Collins (Leeds United)
1966 Bobby Charlton (Manchester United)
1967 Jack Charlton (Leeds United)
1968 George Best (Manchester United)
1969 Tony Book (Manchester City) and
Dave Mackay (Derby County)

1970 Billy Bremner (Leeds United)
1971 Frank McLintock (Arsenal)
1972 Gordon Banks (Stoke City)
1973 Pat Jennings (Tottenham)
1974 Ian Callaghan (Liverpool)
1975 Alan Mullery (Fulham)
1976 Kevin Keegan (Liverpool)
1977 Emlyn Hughes (Liverpool)
1978 Kenny Burns (Nottingham Forest)
1979 Kenny Dalglish (Liverpool)
1980 Terry McDermott (Liverpool)
1981 Frans Thijssen (Ipswich Town)
1982 Steve Perryman (Tottenham)
1983 Kenny Dalglish (Liverpool)
1984 Ian Rush (Liverpool)
1985 Neville Southall (Everton)
1986 Gary Lineker (Everton)
1987 Clive Allen (Tottenham)
1988 John Barnes (Liverpool)

1993

1989

1989 Steve Nicol (Liverpool)
1990 John Barnes (Livepool)
1991 Gordon Strachan (Leeds United)
1992 Gary Lineker (Tottenham)

1993 Chris Waddle (Sheffield Wednesday)
1994 Alan Shearer (Blackburn Rovers)
1995 Jurgen Klinsmann (Tottenham)
1996 Eric Cantona (Manchester United)
1997 Gianfranco Zola (Chelsea)
1998 Dennis Bergkamp (Arsenal)
1999 David Ginola (Tottenham)
2000 Roy Keane (Manchester United)
2001 Teddy Sheringham (Manchester United)
2002 Robert Pires (Arsenal)
2003 Thierry Henry (Arsenal)
2004 Thierry Henry (Arsenal)
2005 Frank Lampard (Chelsea)
2006 Thierry Henry (Arsenal)
2007 Cristiano Ronaldo (Manchester United)
2008 Cristiano Ronaldo (Manchester United)
2009 Steven Gerrard (Liverpool)
2010 Wayne Rooney (Manchester United)
2011 Scott Parker (West Ham)
2012 Robin van Persie (Arsenal)
2013 Gareth Bale (Tottenham)

BAD LADS!

FAMOUS FOOTBALLERS WHO PAID THE PENALTY FOR BREAKING THE RULES...

LUIS SUAREZ

The Liverpool and Uruguay striker was given a ten-game ban in 2013 for biting Chelsea's Branislav Ivanovic. The previous year Suarez was banned for eight-matches after racially abusing Manchester United defender Patrice Evra.

RIO FERDINAND

The England and Man United defender was banned for eight months at the end of 2003 after failing to turn up for a routine drugs test.

ERIC CANTONA

The France forward's legendary kung-fu kick on Crystal Palace fan Matthew Simmons in 1995 earned him a nine-month ban from the game. The Manchester United star was also given 120 hours community service after attacking the Eagles' supporter who had taunted Cantona as he made his way off the pitch.

MARK BOSNICH

The keeper was suspended for nine months after failing a drug test for cocaine in 2002. Aussie Bosnich was sacked by Chelsea.

PAOLO DI CANIO

Now manager of Sunderland, former forward Di Canio was banned for 11 games in September 1998 for pushing referee Paul Alcock while playing for Sheffield Wednesday in the Premier League. The Italian was also fined £10,000.

ROY KEANE

The former Man United and Republic of Ireland captain got a five-week ban and £150,000 fine in 2002 for admitting in his autobiography that he had made a revenge attack on Leeds United's Alf-Inge Haaland.

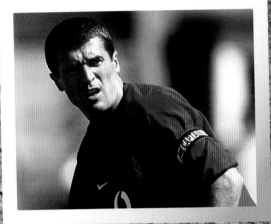

BEN THATCHER

Portsmouth's Pedro Mendes was knocked into advertising boards by Manchester City defender Ben Thatcher in 2006. The Portugal midfielder needed medical attention and Thatcher was banned by City for six games and for eight matches by the Football Association.

DAVID PRUTTON

The midfielder was banned for ten games and fined £6,000 for shoving referee Alan Wiley after being sent-off against Arsenal in 2005, whilst playing for Southampton.

DIEGO MARADONA

Argentina's Diego Maradona served two bans after failing drug tests. In 1991, whilst playing at Napoli, he tested positive for cocaine and was banned for 15 months. Three years later he tested positive for another drug and got a 15-month suspension. He retired in 1997 after failing a further test.

PEPE

Real Madrid defender Pepe pushed Javier Casquero in the penalty box and then kicked the midfielder twice, punched another player and insulted an official. That little episode earned him a ten game ban in 2009. Since then he has stamped on Lionel Messi's hand.

PAUL DAVIS

Arsenal midfielder Davis was banned for nine matches and fined £3,000 after punching Southampton's Glenn Cockerill in 1988.

VINNIE JONES

Hard-man defender turned Hollywood actor Jones was handed a six-month ban in 1992, suspended for three years, and fined a record £20,000 by the FA for taking part in a video on football violence and dirty tricks.

NICOLAS ANELKA

Striker Anelka was banned by France for 18 games following a bust-up with coach Raymond Domenech at the 2010 World Cup finals. The Chelsea star, who was sent home from the finals, announced that he was quitting international football anyway!

ADRIAN MUTU

Chelsea sacked £15m striker Adrian Mutu when he failed a cocaine test and was banned for seven months in 2003. The Romanian also failed a drug test whilst playing for Fiorentina and was handed a nine-month ban which was reduced to six months. In 2011 he was banned for three matches after punching an opposition player.

JOEY BARTON

Midfielder Barton was banned for 12 games, six suspended for two years, after a fight with Man City team-mate Ousmane Dabo in 2007. Barton was also jailed for 74 days the following year after being found guilty of punching a man 20 times in Liverpool.

RENE HIGUITA

Famed for his Scorpion Kick, the Colombia keeper, who was also nicknamed 'The Madman', was banned for six matches in 2004 after testing positive for cocaine. He was also jailed for seven months in 1993 for acting as a go-between for the release of a kidnap victim.

Shoot Football Handbook 2014

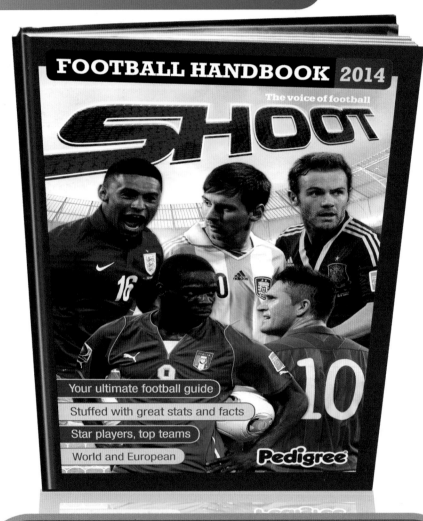

Visit www.pedigreebooks.com

Pedigree Books, Beech Hill House, Walnut Gardens, Exeter EX4 4DH